CAUGHT ON THE TRAIL

Nature's Wildlife Selfies

CAUGHT ON THE TRAIL

NATURE'S WILDLIFE SELFIES

DALE BAKKEN & SANDRA LYNCH-BAKKEN

hancock

house

ISBN-13: 978-0-88839-058-5 [trade edition paperback]
ISBN-13: 978-0-88839-263-3 [epub]

Library and Archives Canada Cataloguing in Publication

Title: Caught on the trail : nature's wildlife selfies / Dale Bakken & Sandra
Lynch-Bakken.
Names: Bakken, Dale, author. | Lynch-Bakken, Sandra, author.
Identifiers: Canadiana (print) 20190236906 | Canadiana (ebook)
20190236914 | ISBN 9780888390585
(softcover) | ISBN 9780888392633 (EPUB)
Subjects: LCSH: Animals—Northwest, Pacific. | LCSH: Animals—North-
west, Pacific—Pictorial works. |
LCSH: Natural history—Northwest, Pacific.
Classification: LCC QL151 .B35 2020 | DDC 591.9795—dc23

Printed in the USA

PRODUCTION & DESIGN: L. Raingam

EDITOR: D. MARTENS

We acknowledge the financial support of the Government of Canada through the Canada Book Fund and the Canada

Council for the Arts, and of the Province of British Columbia through the British Columbia Arts Council and the

Book Publishing Tax Credit.

Hancock House gratefully acknowledges the Semiahmoo, Kwantlen, Katzie, Tsawwassen & Lummi

First Nations, whose unceded traditional territories our offices reside upon.

hancock

house

Published simultaneously in Canada and the United States by

HANCOCK HOUSE PUBLISHERS LTD.
19313 Zero Avenue, Surrey, B.C. Canada V3Z 9R9
#104-4550 Birch Bay-Lynden Rd, Blaine, WA, U.S.A. 98230-9436
(800) 938-1114   Fax (800) 983-2262
www.hancockhouse.com   sales@hancockhouse.com

TABLE OF CONTENTS

INTRODUCTION

Travelling the back country is a popular pass-time in North America. RV's, both mid-size and mega-monsters thunder down our highways on their way to some remote; or semi-remote campsite in search of a wilderness exploit. Cars and vans of all dimensions have their trunks and roof racks crammed with gear; kayaks, bikes, tents, camp stoves, coolers and fishing poles all bungie strapped into place. As they leave behind their urban neighbourhoods these adventurers share one common goal: to escape the chaos of everyday life to find solitude wrapped nicely in a package labelled NATURE. And although they may know little about the wild they are induced to fashion their spare time around it.

Hundreds of thousands of people make the trek to the great outdoors every year. Some are primed and set for what they may come up against, while others venture recklessly into a world they think they know because they saw it on Facebook, or Googled it, or someone texted them about an awesome trail they should check-out. I am buffaloed by the unpreparedness of such people. Ignorance is blind as they say, or could seriously end in blindness if they are not vigilant as to what is around the next bend on the footpath.

So, as the masses enter the domain of the dense wooded forest, the rugged mountain trail, the turbulent salmon streams and the white waters of rushing rivers the adventurer should be aware of what lives there. It is a place that has little to no cell reception, no street lights, no neon directional signs and no traffic turmoil - just the sounds of the wild as it breathes.

As children of the baby boomer era, we were fortunate because progress hadn't yet raped endless green patches and replaced them with another shopping mall, cul-de-sac community, parking lot, convenience store or drive-through restaurant. We grew up with a rich abundance of nature just outside our window, and learned early-on how to co-exist with wildlife. We made angels-in-the-snow right next to gray partridge as they buried themselves under winter's blanket. A walk to school was safe but slow, since we always spotted some small creature that needed further investigating: leopard frogs half submerged in a rain puddle (now listed as threatened in some parts of Canada), a red-backed salamander slithering toward a patch of moss, a fledgling blue bird looking helpless on the ground, or an eastern cottontail munching on sweet clover and needing to grow-up fast to outrun and outmaneuver enemy raptors and bobcats.

Our play-stations weren't hand-held devices. They were the common garter snakes that lived under our porch. They were the badgers and Richardson's ground squirrels that shared the same farmland - both predator and prey excavating earth mounds. When we ventured too close to the guard ground squirrel it would send the colony scurrying for the safety of the burrows with its shrill alarm cry, sometimes tragically to find a badger awaiting their return. The white-tailed deer and her speckled fawn that nibbled on new shoots adjacent to the chicken coop was always a favourite sight, but the caterpillars that fed on the milkweed plant and eventually morphed into the golden-hued beauty we know as the monarch butterfly taught us patience and gentleness as we tried our best to coax one to land on our hand. When we failed, as we often did, we turned our skills to the competitive game of skipping rocks on the water as surface-feeding ducks like redheads (their numbers also disappearing) and pintail dived for food, with only their feathered bottoms visible, bobbing above the water like a cork.

But the best play-station of all was our make-shift tree house, where we lay on our bellies and peered across the field at a fox vixen play with her young kits. We were her admiring audience as she and her babies kept us entertained. And admission was always free.

Wildlife was our neighbour, and we thought it quite natural to have it so. Our morning alarm clock was the songbirds' symphony, and we were lulled to sleep by the far-carrying hoots of great horned owls and croaking bullfrogs. We were a lucky generation, because we grew up with wildlife drama playing-out all around us and in the nearby woods, with their carpet of white trilliums seducing us to enter the magical forest, or at least as magical as it seemed in our childhood minds.

Our parents taught us to watch and learn how Mother Nature raised her family, so both animals and humans could grow old alongside one another.

BAKKEN

To those of us now considered seniors, it is quite ludicrous when we see television commercials advertise "let's bring back play" - something that should be innate in every youngster. But that's where the 21st century has brought us. We can boast triumph at turning children into sedentary, overweight lumps and depleting countless species from all orders because of a profound change in our world: mercury in the water, air pollution, massive habitat loss, ultraviolet light exposure, disease and the introduction of invasive species.

Sadly, mornings are much quieter these days, as the fields have been silenced and the forest no longer has a song. Mockingbirds have disappeared as their habitat has changed and is far more conducive for robins. The vireo's meadow has been flooded, and the river that acted as a beacon for hummingbirds, cedar waxwings, willow flycatchers and meadowlarks has dried up. A line from Advocacy for Animals (Encyclopedia Britannica) says it best: "Songbirds are the proverbial canaries in the great coal mines that are the environment."

Most of this century's plant and animal invaders were launched by human activities. Some are so notable they deserve mention. First on the list of trespassers is the mountain pine beetle. It has decimated 16 million hectares of pine forests in British Columbia alone. Climate change is the prime culprit that spawns this destructive invertebrate. Our unusually hot, dry summers and mild winters have altered the beetle's life cycle and allowed it to continue with its voracious appetite. The affected hillsides are no longer covered in a wall of lush emerald green, but instead are ravaged - bald stands of umber.

The introduction of red-eared slider terrapins, a non-indigenous species in this country, but a big seller in pet-stores, has led to domination of our ponds and lakes, where western and eastern painted turtles once lived. Irresponsible pet owners simply release them into nearby waterways when the reptile has outgrown its fish bowl and the child has outgrown the novelty.

And lastly are foreign noxious wildflowers and weeds that have escaped their intended gardens or landscape. They choke out native vegetation and in doing so destroy vital wildlife habitat. They decrease crop quality and volume, reduce soil stability, provide a haven for insects and diseases, are the source of physical irritation to passersby due to prickles, spines and burrs, and they replace the manicured aesthetic look of landscapes with unsightly sprawl.

Among these plunderers is giant hogweed, also known as giant cow parsnip. Perhaps the 1962 horror movie, 'The Day of the Triffids' was inspired by this five-metre-high plant. Its stem hairs and leaves contain a clear, septic sap that when touched can cause the skin to burn and form pustules leaving behind scars. It has a vigorous early-season growth, a tolerance for full shade canopy, and even seasonal flooding proves to be no match. The *Heracleum mantegazzianum* is one tough perennial. It's standing up to its name *Herculese*.

The parrot's feather is another enemy. As a popular choice at garden centres for people's aquariums and outdoor ponds, this duo submersed/emergent *Myriophyllum aquaticum* has spread into natural bodies of water. It can out-compete and replace native water vegetation, and in doing so creates pools of stagnant water - ideal breeding ground for mosquitos. Be prepared to stock up on bug repellent.

But an introduced species that really carries a punch, or in this case a sting, is the European fire ant. Its maiden voyage to North American's eastern seaboard from its native Eurasia was in the 1900s. This insect will attack aggressively if intruded upon. It will pinch down with its mandible then swing around and sting multiple times. People have died of anaphylactic shock (severe allergic reaction) after being stung by these nasty *Myrmica rubra*.

The odds are clearly stacked against nature to maintain a hold on her once pristine biodiversity. Nevertheless, when she is victorious we humans are enriched with pockets of wildlife still intact. These places become our target spots for holiday and weekend retreats.

This book is a glimpse into what still roams wild and a testament to nature's resilience. Even with humanity's continued abuse of this beautiful Earth there is still life beating deep within the forest and on the edge of our urban communities. Take a stroll through these pages and cherish what can still be found out there if we choose to walk gently in their tracks and leave little trace of ourselves. If we do that, then they stand a chance to continue to wow us into the future.

We are not the only species on this planet, so join us as we celebrate some of the others.

CHAPTER 1

TRAIL CAMERA LOW-DOWN

As far back as the 1800s, photography buffs have tried to capture wildlife doing natural behaviour in their natural habitat. The times and technology have undeniably changed, from trip-wire activation, bulky camera bodies and still camera film usage to what is now available.

Every image throughout these pages, with the exception of a handful, was taken using a trail camera: also known as a - game cam and camera trap. What's important to note is that no person was at the helm tripping the shutter. Essentially, the wildlife took the photo – selfies, if you wish. I guess you could say these cameras were the trailblazer to selfie taking long before the "I'll take a picture of myself" mania erupted.

There are no definitive pros and cons to remote camera usage. It comes down to your personal belief and the purpose for operating one as to whether you argue for or against. We will touch upon who uses them and leave it to you to decide if that is a pro or con. For us, it's simple. When they are utilized to allow and assist wildlife to survive, then more usage of them is better.

The following points are incentives for selecting these cameras, which assuredly will unite the pro and con sides. Such as camera will never stop shooting because it needs to relieve itself, stretch its legs because it has sat cramped too long in a blind, because it's being mobbed by mosquitoes and blackflies, or the weather is too gnarly to be out in. Nor will it emit a scent or sound that could alert the animal to its presence, or have to call it a day because the sun has set. Without a doubt, such a camera is the perfect bush buddy if you want to photograph nocturnal, diurnal, nervous, aggressive, shy, elusive, solitary or highly vigilant wildlife, all in the comforts of your home. It allows you to outwit their keen senses and come away with some amazing pictures, rain or shine.

Since humans are predators – animals that seem to forget we are animals, these cameras were introduced to the hunting enthusiast at sporting goods stores. They're still a major purchase item at those outlets. Cabela's website alone has seven pages filled with nothing but trail cams. Hunters use them to inventory the quantity, age and size of game animals, thereby pinpointing their desired animal destined for the dinner table. It also assists the trapper in locating and identifying the fur-bearing animal condemned as a fashion item. These cameras are so effective, the hunter/trapper can strategically place a mineral lick, bait station, snare or trap precisely in the optimum spot to ambush the animal and finish it off.

They are simply part of the arsenal used to up the odds of the hunter coming away with his quarry, alongside night-vision goggles, blinds, game calls, whistles, decoys, high-powered rifles with their scopes, and all-terrain vehicles which gain them access into those tough-to-get-to places. Whatever it takes to make the hunt less difficult and tiresome, and to guarantee success? One way to view all these extra advantages is that they are cheating and unethical. Maybe it's time to start arming the animals to make it fairer. It's just a thought.

It's not just the hunting community that uses these cameras, however. They also play a major role in wildlife management by researchers and field biologists. This enables them to observe and learn more, so as to accurately measure herd densities and doe-to-buck ratios, as well as obtain essential data to create wildlife corridors and so forth. The cameras provide pertinent details to wildlife professionals, akin to radio telemetry, on the movements of targeted individuals of grizzlies and wolves by picking up each animal's unique electromagnetic radio signal given off by a transmitter attached to a collar.

Originating back in the 1960s, radio-collaring has turned a positive into a very ugly negative. It has allowed B.C. biologist gunners to home in on the co-ordinates of a specific collared wolf and shoot the entire pack from helicopters, killing hundreds (roughly 268 over the past two decades) - quick, easy and completely legal because it has been authorized by our provincial government. What they don't want you to know is that it is not done humanely or painlessly. Right from the get go, the low flying helicopter terrorizes the animal, and once it's in the sniper's scope the wolf often dies violently, with multiple bullets or strangling snares. Those animals that manage to elude the flying fiend disperse, leaving the wolf family ripped apart. The collapse of the pack has lasting deleterious effects on the remaining members.

Anytime some new device or technology is developed, there is always the possibility it could be used to harm instead of benefit. That is the human design.

Returning to the trail camera, there is a story worthy of mention, one where a camera made the difference between life and death. Bear biologist Dr. Lynn Rogers and his partner spent hours on - foot searching throughout an eighty-acre forest without locating a 5-month-old cub born to his case study bear 'Lily', who had become separated from her mother.

Weeks went by with no sign of the little one they named 'Hope'. Killed was the only conclusion they felt possible. Nonetheless, unwilling to give up, they set up a trail camera next to a tree where the cub had often climbed to retreat from danger. It was a long shot, but long shots occur every day, so why not for a tiny bear cub? Then the photo they had set their hearts on appeared. Gloom shifted to joy and reconfirmed they had picked the perfect name for this resilient, little bear. She had beaten the odds and survived torrential thunderstorms, predators, the spring bear hunt and her lack of knowledge as to where to find food in late spring and early summer. As she peered around a tree trunk, looking thin, but very much alive, the camera snapped a shot of her sweet face. Rogers had left grapes at the bottom of the tree in the off- chance Hope might show up and find food she no doubt was in desperate need of. His decision to intervene, although controversial and met with criticism, saved the animal's life. We applaud him for that. Humans intervene for human life all the time. The same should hold true for animals.

Each day, around the same time, Hope appeared on the camera eager to eat whatever had been left there. Where she went and how she stayed safe the other hours of the day remained a mystery? Eventually, Dr. Rogers was able to kennel her and return her to her mother. The reunion between mother and cub was pure bliss, with Hope immediately finding a teat to suckle - strengthening their bond. 'The Bear Family & Me' is a BBC documentary that filmed this bear family story and highlights Dr. Rogers' ground-breaking work with black bears.

From Minnesota to the Florida Everglades to northern British Columbia to Glacier National Park, these cameras are imperative if one is to locate, document and photograph some of nature's most secretive creatures, like the one mentioned next.

One highly notable research team which has gathered much of its biological information through the eye of a remote camera is the Wolverine Project. Our wolverine photographs are also case in point. We would never have been treated to such entrancing images if these cameras had not been set up. Nor would we even have been aware wolverines are still out there roaming this mountain range. What a naturalist's ultimate high.

Even rarer than the wolverine is what the following group uses these cameras for. The Big Foot Research Group hopes to snap pictures of the legionary Sasquatch to support their claim and steadfast belief these creatures do exist. Needless to say, we were over the top with excitement when our camera took just such a picture at our apple tree on the front lawn. Or is it some altogether different creature? You tell us.

Aside from these usages, similar cameras are used for home security systems and nanny cams, which are - both motion activated. These are great ways to keep an eye-out for Christmas decoration hooligans, finding out who is thrashing through your lovely flowerbed, or checking -up on the babysitter and the kids during your absence, in case they do something that bears witness to the saying "kids will be kids."

In conjunction with all of these modes is one final use: lost pets. An animal might run off because of a loud, frightening noise (thunder/firecrackers), a car accident, or an encounter with a prey or predator animal (chasing or being chased). When the pet is no longer at the end of the leash, within the confines of the backyard, or within calling distance, remote cameras work quite well.

This story is a prime example. It was nearing dusk, on a summer afternoon, when one of our eight indoor cats slipped out the front door without being seen, and when faced with the scary outdoors bolted for the nearby woods. Our endless calling did nothing to coax her back to us. We weren't even sure she was close enough to hear our calls. From the time she was a kitten, she'd been an inside cat, and a nervous one at that, so we were doubly worried how she'd fare out there. Days went by and still no Jingles. We came to accept she was gone for good, but decided to set up a remote camera by the house next to the food dish we had put out for her. The dish was always empty by morning, but visited by what we didn't know. Hopefully the camera would answer that.

To our utter relief, she arrived at the camera that very night around midnight, shortly after the racoons had eaten their fill. To our disappointment, though, this went on for two more long weeks, and with large predators in the area our worry was legitimate. For reasons unknown, she chose to flee to the woods instead of staying near the house after she ate. It was evident her flight response was stronger than the stay-put-and-be-exposed alternative. The forest provided that safety. Her level of fear was so intense it even kept her from coming to me during daylight hours when I'd call and call. The only way to rescue her was to set a live trap next to the food. But this presented new problems.

We didn't want to trap racoons, or any other animal for that matter, plus her scared state made her even wary of the metal box that suddenly appeared. Several more days went by before she accepted that the object wasn't going to harm her. Bit by bit, she became accustomed to it being there, which allowed us to open the trap door and place the food dish just inside - first at its entrance and then toward the back. Patience was the key to making this work.

Eureka! We finally got her. Pressed tight against the back wire wall and with eyes the size of paws, she cowered. Even my familiar voice didn't soothe her. We threw a blanket over the trap and carried her inside the house. She ping-ponged off all four sides until the cage was set down. We flipped the trap door open and Bug, her best buddy, promptly sauntered inside to investigate and greet her. He had what it took. She followed him out where the other six cats surrounded her - nuzzle here, a lick there and a sniff everywhere. They probably wondered why she smelled so strange, and where she'd been all this time. The cat clan welcomed her home.

So if you are ever confronted with a lost or runaway pet, try setting up a camera in an area you believe the animal may return to, and bait it with its favourite foods. You're likely to get something else eating the meal, which is always intriguing, but if you're lucky your beloved pet will come into view.

Now - back to the use of trail cameras for wildlife viewing. Over the years we have set-up various brands of trail cameras. Some have the bells and whistles, while others are quite basic. The cameras are left on the trails month after month, year round, and have functioned well in the winter at temperatures colder than -25 degrees Celsius. On average they are in the mid-price range of $100 to $300. Most trail cams are priced around $100 to $600, whereas the Reconyx has wireless models listed for over $1000. We have successfully captured well over a thousand images, of which this book exhibits but a fraction of those.

Trail camera development and technology has made leaps and bounds in the past decade, with improved battery life, faster trigger speeds, recovery times, increase detection, flash range, improved picture quality, as well as lenses so sharp they can count the winter ticks on a moose's neck. Though - sadly, some of those wretched ticks are the size of moth balls, so even a crappy camera could see them.

Video resolution can vary greatly among cameras, and if video is important to you, then, be sure to choose wisely. Many manufacturers offer wireless technology that can shoot colour photos and video with audio in night-time conditions. The latest trail cameras have a certain level of adjustability - some more than others. Know what your camera is capable of, and your camera's various capture modes and sensitivity adjustments. Don't be afraid to experiment with settings. You have a lot more play with these cameras than you may think. Determine what your needs are and match a camera to those features.

There is growing hype over faster trigger speeds, recovery times, higher megapixels and different flash options. Most of this is just that - hype and marketing. Some of our best photos have come from cameras with relatively run-of-the-mill features. Placement of your camera is everything. To up-the-odds that your subject will be in the centre of the frame when the shot is taken, contemplate what animal you are hoping to photograph and its physical height, and in doing so, tilt the camera accordingly, otherwise you may end up with these types of photos: - a partial arm and chest of a cub trying to mess with the camera, or an inquisitive squirrel on his way up the tree.

For transient mammals it becomes trickier, as they don't tend to stop and pose. They are on the move up and down the trails, so, gauging from what direction they will be arriving, and how fast, is anyone's guess. So long as you place your cameras on obvious wildlife trails, your luck will improve over time. Having said that, - even with careful placement invariably you will end up with either the hind end of the animal, or just its legs (as is the case with many of our moose photos), or just its head. The animal may be too close and out-of-focus, or the entire animal is blurred, which more often than not occurs with our lynx images. It is a difficult cat to get quality pictures of, which is baffling, because typically it doesn't move that quickly, but evidently fast enough to cause the camera to obscure him/her. And then you have the recurrent photos where there is zilch in the picture, leaving you to wonder: Did something move at Mach speed, or did the camera simply malfunction?

All these elements make using these cameras a challenge, yet a gratifying one. There are no guarantees you will come away with much to be thrilled over, but then again, you could. You are not in a studio setting under perfect lighting next to a prop waiting for the subject to be placed precisely where you want them. Wildlife moves in and out of territories daily, seasonally, - it varies, but that's what makes capturing a picture of wild fauna such a thrill when it happens.

With the proper location and appropriate backgrounds, you will be amazed with the images you will be rewarded with – maybe. Remember, I said there are NO guarantees. But be patient, because sometimes you come away with stunning photos purely by luck. We want to emphasize, always be aware of any clutter - objects that may cloud, or distract in the photo; an overhanging branch that may cause a shadow, any tall vegetation, or a camera position that's too low, or too high, or with a horizon that's off.

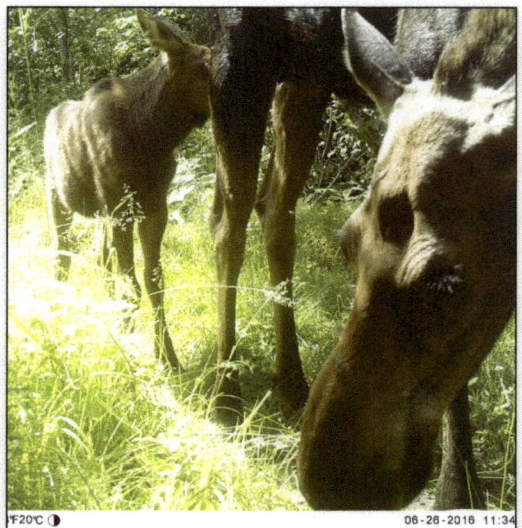

Again, we need to mention that since these cameras are motion activated, even when you go to great lengths to remove any unwanted obstacle in the camera's sightline, you must be

ready for numerous photos devoid of your desired subject. All you end-up with is a slight variation of the same scene because the pesky wind took charge that day and caused an adjacent leaf or branch to move sufficiently enough to trigger the device. Your excitement at having captured hundreds of pictures quickly shifts to a letdown. You find you only have a few images that actually have what you were hopeful of getting, while the rest are duds that you now have to painstakingly scan through and delete. The wind is a crafty component tough to control. The sun, on the other hand, is more compliant, moving across the sky on its predictable path, which enables you to predetermine if and when it could shine directly into the camera, resulting in a washout. You can therefore make adjustments to eliminate those botched pictures.

MOVING ONWARD WITH THE LOW-DOWN:
- It is not a high number of megapixels that gives you a good quality picture, but rather the quality of the camera lens. Megapixels have turned into useless numbers through modern day marketing ploys. Our advice? Just forget them.
- Trigger speeds and recovery times have turned into numbers measured by the 1/100th of a second. Think about it. Does that really matter? Remember, these animals are not breaking the sound barrier while travelling the trails.
- Battery life is extremely vital if you have several cameras and/or you leave them out for extended periods of time in all weather conditions. On the other hand, for the person with one camera that uses multiple AA batteries that may not be a concern.
- Detection range is important. It should provide both a wide angle and good range of depth. This detection angle is a V-shape spreading out from the lens of your camera. Try to visualize this V when setting up your camera and how it relates to where you position it in the field in relation to natural objects and open areas.
- Flash options and range. There is a great deal of muttering over which is better, and what scares off the animals and whatnot. You have low glow, no glow and white flash, with probably more options and variables on the way. Buy what you like and what suits your desired outcome. Some

flashes give very poor quality photos due to lack of light. Some flashes and camera range are so extreme you end up with a picture of an animal at such a vast distance, why even bother? Some will give you horrid eye shine that is as blinding as a car with its high beams on.

- One thing we would like to de-bunk is that white flash or a noisy camera trigger scares off the animal. This is completely false, at least from our experience. As you've seen with some of the photographs, the animal's curiosity actually gave us some wonderfully funny close-up shots. The animal could see the white flash and came in closer and stayed longer.

Perhaps we are just lucky in that the wildlife in our remote area are not hunted and have not been harassed by humans and therefore are less wary and more inquisitive.

- Placement. Where you set the camera is paramount. Be aware of the sun's movement in order to avoid having the camera shoot directly into bright daylight, which will give you washout conditions and make it impossible to see your subject. In addition, look around at anything that might cast a large shadow and give your picture a dark background and a near invisible object.

- Camera warranty. Over a decade ago, these cameras were highly durable and indestructible and would last for years. Nowadays, the newer models, although equipped with more features, are made with cheap plastic parts, and the warranties tend to be only one to two years. Coincidently they also seem to malfunction just past the warranty life, inaugurating them into our world of disposable mania. So be buyer-savvy and purchase a camera with at least a two-year warranty from a reputable manufacturer.

- We only use Duracell alkaline batteries, contradiction to what manufactures often recommend, which are the more expensive battery types. We believe

it is not necessary. Generally we use 4B to 16GB class 4 SD cards. We find higher class 6 and class 10 cards are a waste of money, with no real value for the extra money spent. For field work we find it important that the camera we choose uses a full-size SD card. A micro SD or TF card is more difficult to remove from the camera and change out in the field.

Here is an inventory of trail cameras we have used in the past fifteen years: **Apeman** 12MP 1080P, **Bushnell** Trophy Cam XLT, 8MP Trophy Cam HD, 12 MP Trophy Cam Essential Low Glow, **Cuddeback, ScoutGuard** SG560-8M, SG560P, SG565F-8M, SG860C-12MHD and Moultrie I45, I60, Panoramic 150, MCG 13201 A series, **Rexway** 720P and **Wildgame** Innovations Terra 5, TX 10I1-8 Terra Extreme.

We have found each brand and model has an ideal function unique to that camera. Know your camera models and what they are proficient at and what their weaknesses are, and use that to your photo-capture advantage.

We never hard-mount any of our cameras to trees, but instead use a Pedco Ultra-Pod II tripod in the folded position, then Velcro it back onto itself, or a generic swivel mount, whereby the base is screwed to the tree and the camera screwed into the swivel head of the mount. The pivoting head of the Ultra-Pod is used to direct the camera aim. We found if a bear swats the camera for whatever reason it will do far less damage if the camera is free to pivot or swivel. This happened with one cub. With another bear it pulled the camera off the tree, chewed the outer casing until it satisfied its inquisitiveness, then, discarded it into the bushes. Surprisingly, we were still able to use it after the bruin had his fun with it. If the camera is hard-mounted, chances are it will be totally destroyed if the bear is intent on removing it.

To sum up: Run out and get yourself a trail camera, and let the adventure begin. You might be utterly shocked what varmint is ambling by your house, your backyard or your cabin while you sleep. It could be four-legged or two. But for now, let us show you what ambled by on our trails.

CHAPTER 2

AUTUMNS' ACCESSORIES

With the onset of autumn comes a sense of urgency for all species. Humans flip from carefree summer romps to a state of mayhem as they scuttle about, buying their children new outfits and equipping them with all the trimmings necessary for the new school year. Summer clothes are stored to make room for knitted garments. Homes are winterized. Logs for wood-burning stoves are stockpiled. Vehicle tires are rotated and engine lubricants topped off. And the labour of love in the vegetable garden throughout the summer has produced a sizable amount of fare that gardeners now pull and meticulously prepare and store in freezers or cold cellars.

Wildlife is somewhat similar. The pace of animals is also hastened as they scout for suitable den sites and, feverishly stash food in tree nooks. Birds of every size and colour gather to communicate their migrating plans, hyperphagia registers within all bears, and the compulsion to breed reaches its crest for hoofed mammals.

As the deciduous trees enter into dormancy and their leaves begin to die, they celebrate one final hurrah, which is a gift to any onlooker. It is a visual pageant with vibrant hues of crimson and gold blotting the landscape. But all good things must come to an end, and soon nakedness replaces the arboreal splendor as each leaf falls from its host onto the forest floor, giving up remnant nutrients to the soil, where it all began, and will begin again. Despite what we may think, nature is not quite done aweing the viewer, for there are other lavish accessories to be seen. And it is the moose that reigns as the ungulate monarch of the forest, and boasts the most imperial of all accessories.

MOOSE

The name *moose* is extracted from an Algonquian word that means "eater of twigs" - precisely what (*Alces alces*) does.

Habitat

Close to a million roam the forests of Canada, Alaska and the northern strata of the lower forty-eight United States. The tundra, boreal forests with their wetlands, and shallow ponds and lakes with mixed hardwood and coniferous trees are home to moose. They offer ample willows, aspen, white birch, balsam fir, spruce, assorted herbs and shrubs, and aquatic vegetation. Where there is food like this, there are moose.

The Rut

All male ungulates are adorned with either antlers or horns. Some are more jaw-dropping than others. This moose wasn't a contender in the jaw-dropping contest. Nevertheless, they are an accessory that, once dried-up and dropped-off, often is turned into a work of art: antler chandeliers, for example. A moose rack converts to a canvass for a painting, and carvings are created out of antler bone. But before being transformed into some ornament, these prized accessories serve a serious purpose. Essentially they are a billboard to female

ungulates, to show just how virile and worthy their owner is to breed with her. They also publicize to other males that this male is prepared for a showdown if challenged.

The rutting season intrigues us humans, for it is when Mother Nature flaunts her autumn colours, flexes her muscles in the gleaming September sun, or moonlit-night, and hormones run rampant – not unlike what occurs at many fitness gyms.

Bull moose begin every winter with two new small knots of soft tissue forming on each side of the head. These knots are called pedicels. From their minuscule beginnings, they erupt into what a hunter dreams of hanging above their garage door - an expression of pure machoism.

A bull moose in his prime (five to ten years of age) can display an impressive five-foot-wide rack of hardened bone, can stand seven-feet-tall at the shoulders, have roughly a forty-inch-long leg, and weigh in at up to 1,400 pounds. During the rut this formidable animal is highly unpredictable and extremely bad-tempered.

I was once chased through the bush by a bull moose in Algonquin Provincial Park in Ontario solely because I was in his territory, and he viewed me as an annoyance. If he could have caught up to me I have no doubt he would have stomped me into the ground. It was only when I was safe inside my car that the crushing pain in my chest stopped. I am no Olympic runner, but I sure ran for the gold that day.

The Boone and Crockett Club's big game records cite an Alaskan bull's rack weighing seventy-seven pounds, and another bull's rack measuring over eighty-one inches across. That would be comparable to strapping a seven-foot-long railroad tie on top of your head. Needless to say, you would require massive neck muscles and unwavering balance so as not to face-plant into the dirt.

The first phase of the moose rut, which commences on August 25 (give-or-take a day), according to seasoned moose researcher Victor Van Ballenberghe, is the shedding of the dried-up-velvet. Some moose have been known to eat the bloody tatters that dangle from their antlers. The once- sensitive velvet antlers, which they are careful not to nudge, or damage as blood threads through them, are replaced by calcified bone prepared to do battle with each and every rival. This moose is nearing the stage of shedding his velvet.

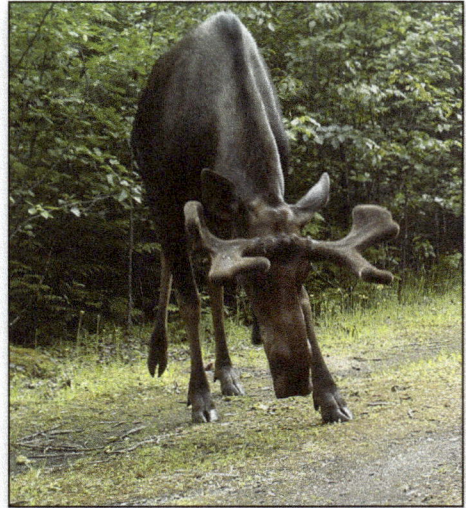

By September, the mating season is well under way. September 11-25 marks the start of phase two. During this time, bulls pursue cows with dogged determination. As they wander their forested home, their grunts can be heard. Unlike bull elk, which gather a harem and prevent cows from leaving the group, bull moose do not control the cows.

At the peak of the rut, bulls high on testosterone, seem to lose all sense of scale and safety. The following documented encounter supports this. The animal believed it could take on any comers. He stood his ground and stared down his opponent, but the train just kept coming. In Norway, 30 percent of the 1,500 to 2,000 moose traffic deaths each year are caused by trains. In some of those cases, the animal was trapped on the track in deep cuttings through the mountains and couldn't get away.

A more hazardous situation is when the snow is so deep it prevents the moose from escaping to the side of the track. A moose, no matter how large or ornery, is no match for a train, despite what its hormones are telling it.

Every hour in Canada, four to eight large animal-vehicle collisions take place. It is estimated that there are 45,000 animal-vehicle collisions each year. This figure is growing at an alarming rate of 10 to 15 percent. The statistics in a Transport Canada Road Safety report shows the seriousness of the situation for both motorists and wildlife. And although collisions can happen at any time, the peak hours seem to be between 10 p.m. and midnight.

Disease

Once the rut is over, moose must then contend

with winter. But it is not just the hardship of the season; besides finding sufficient food to sustain their body core temperature and maintain necessary layers of fat, they must also deal with parasites.

The brain or meningeal worm kills moose and other ungulates. The worm's life cycle begins in deer and involves a temporary stay in a snail or slug. The adult worm lives in and on the nervous tissues and meninges that coat the brain, and there they lay eggs in the blood vessels. The eggs travel to the lungs through the blood stream, where they hatch to larvae, which are in turn coughed-up or swallowed and passed in feces. On the ground, they attach themselves to a snail/slug, which attaches itself to vegetation, which in turn the deer eats. These gastropods travel through the blood to the spinal cord and eventually to the tissue of the brain, where the cycle begins all over again. The same vegetation that houses these snails/slugs is eaten by moose, and once in the moose's body, the worm migrates through the spinal cord and brain. Directly infected, things go from bad to worse for the moose - it becomes disoriented, staggers about, can go blind, collapses and dies.

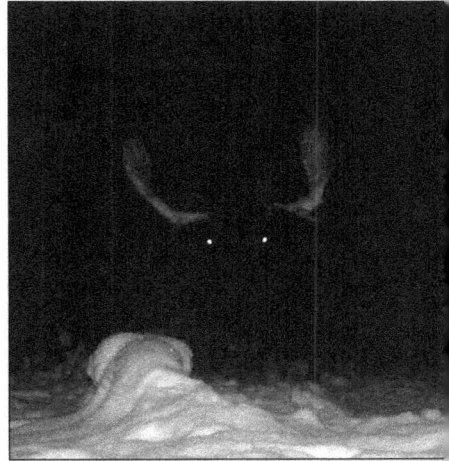

Dr. Jerry Haigh, a well-known veterinarian, once described a moose captured on video in the final stage of this disease before death: "It was a grim session, and I could not watch all the way through the second time."

A true enemy to the moose is the winter tick. As the name might imply, it thrives in our Canadian winters. But its cycle begins in the fall. It will latch onto any passing moose and stay warmly tucked in the insulating hairs throughout the cold months, sucking and gorging a meal of blood. With spring's arrival, the female blood-filled tick drops from its host and lays thousands of eggs. These eggs remain dormant during the hot months, but then hatch into six-legged, pin-head-sized larvae, that ascend the vegetation and form small clumps. These clumps wriggle their legs around, waiting to grab on to the next passer-by. It's interesting how the positioning of these small clumps is smack-dab at the body core height of moose and elk. Clever little ticks. They live out the rest of their lives on the host animal.

The diseased moose becomes gravely emaciated and, has massive hair loss, primarily in the neck and shoulder region. The coat turns a light colour, giving such animals the nickname of "ghost moose." An affected moose can be home to 40,000 ticks. A female tick can take 2mml of blood per day. If half of the ticks on the host animal are females, that equates to 40 litres of sucked blood from the moose. Plainly put, a 400 kg moose that only has a total blood volume of 32 litres suffers greatly to replace the energy-rich substance.

In addition, these ticks cause their host terrible irritation, so the moose expends a great deal of time grooming, which distracts from normal feeding behaviour at a time when the animal is already trying to cope with the hardships of the snow, cold and diminished quantities of nutrient- rich vegetation. Although this moose didn't suffer from winter ticks, several invasive growths are seen on its legs and shoulder area, which feasibly hindered its overall health.

How to Stay Safe

If you come upon a bull during the rut, be sure he knows you are there. They have poor eyesight, so talk quietly to let him know you are not an adversary, but an eager human wanting to take a photo, or a distracted hiker who mistakenly took the path he had claimed. Quickly find a tree to climb or hide behind, and above all else, give him plenty of space. His grunts and bellows, along with a lowered head displaying his rack, followed by him swaying his antlers back and forth, are a clear message that he wants you gone and to stop interrupting his courtship game plan.

Did You Know?

It is often said "moose have a face only a mother could love." I must disagree. I find a moose's face quite enchanting. Perhaps that stems from my childhood years of watching 'Rocky and Bullwinkle' on television.

COYOTE

These carnivores' autumn accessories are not flamboyant like those of the moose, and in fact are rather mundane. They come in the form of camouflage. Their pelage takes on the tones of its surrounding - flaxen and umber, nothing flashy.

Brush wolf, God's dog, yodeler, American jackal and prairie wolf are all nicknames given to one crafty predator - the coyote. There are nineteen subspecies of coyote; the one that ranges through the Yukon, the Northwest Territories, northern British Columbia, northern Alberta and Alaska is the *Canis latrans incolatus*.

Habitat

These canids range throughout much of North America and into Central America, from the grasslands, to forests, to the foothills and mountains to sagebrush terrain. Being highly adaptive, they are also showing up more frequently in large cities as humans take over more of their natural habitat. Its wide distribution may someday take it as far as South America, as it is already present beyond the Panama Canal.

Characteristics

The coyote's size varies depending on what geographical region it occupies. Northern subspecies tend to be larger, weighing on average 18 kg (39

pounds) whereas the southern subspecies of Mexico only weigh around 11.5 kg (25 pounds). Their body lengths run about 1.35 metres, with a tail length of 40 centimetres. The largest coyote on record was back in 1937. It was a male killed near Afton, Wyoming, that weighed

a whopping 33.9 kg (75 pounds). From his nose to the tip of his tail he measured 1.6 metres – huge in coyote terms.

Generally it is easy to distinguish a coyote from a wolf: as a rule they are smaller overall. Its narrow face, muzzle and jaws lack the grasping power necessary to hold the large prey that wolves tend to target. To further validate

how inferior their biting power is to that of a wolf, their sagittal crest is lower or entirely flat. Coyotes' molars also show a larger chewing surface, denoting their comparative reliance on vegetation. When running or walking they carry their tail downwards, whereas wolves' tails are horizontal. Their scent gland, although smaller, is located in the same vicinity as a wolf's: - upper side of the base of the tail and bluish black in colour.

A coyote's coat is predominantly light gray and tawny with black and white streaks throughout, except in the fall when they blend well with tree foliage. In northern high- elevation areas they have more gray and black shades than their fellow desert-dwellers, which are more whitish-gray. In keeping with the consumer's lust for fur in the 1860s, when beaver pelts diminished the coyote pelt took its place, and by the 1950s paid out $5 to $25per pelt. These were primarily used for trimmings on coat collars and sleeves. Often they were dyed black to replicate that of a silver fox.

Behaviour

Unlike wolves, coyotes are more solitary then gregarious, albeit in winter they do turn social, forming small, loose-knit hunting packs of non-family individuals to readily find food, and bring down prey too large for a single attacker. Often, but not always, these social groups are temporary, and consist of bachelor males, sub-adult young and non-breeding females. In these summer photos we had a pair, (uncertain of their sex), wander together for several days.

Speed is of huge benefit to coyotes, capable of running 64 kilometers an hour, as there are times they are forced to travel up to 160 km (100 miles) to find food when their home range is overpopulated, making prey scarce. Since they don't typically defend their territory beyond the denning season, they are far less aggressive toward an interloper than the wolf is, and though they do fight and put trespassers to flight, death rarely occurs.

Diet/Hunting

Originally, they were thought to be strict carnivores, but in fact they are omnivores, making both meat and vegetation part of their diet. They are not discerning eaters. Their food choice can run from small snakes all the way up the ladder to large game animals and everything in between - frogs, insects, rodents, fish, birds, rabbits, fruit and grass, although there does seem to be evidence they don't fancy shrews, moles, toads or brown rats. In cities, coyotes rely heavily on pet food and garbage to stay alive. Cannibalism is part of their survival; they will, readily eat the carcasses of conspecifics. In fact, coyote hunters once used coyote fat to either lure

the animal in or laced the bait with poison, knowing the animal would approach.

Akin to the wolf, coyotes have earned the title of vermin, one reason being that they prey on pets and livestock. So if your local, feral cat colony begins to lessen, chances are the coyote's belly is full - a very good reason for keeping your cat indoors.

Olfactory has long been considered their primary sense used for hunting. Yet recent research contradicts that. Researchers investigated the role of auditory, visual and olfactory senses and discovered that visual cues were in fact the most important ones used by coyotes when they hunt. When coyotes go after large ungulates, they do it either in pairs or small groups, and factors such as snow depth and crust density determines whether they succeed or fail to kill. Unlike the wolf that attacks from the rear, coyotes do a frontal attack, tearing at the prey's head and throat. Hunting porcupines is a pairs-game. They use their paws to flip the animal onto its back, then, attack its soft underbelly. Young coyotes invariably come away with quill injuries, but experienced adults have the technique perfected.

Breeding

The breeding season is between February and March. When the female enters estrous she will scent-mark and repeatedly howl to draw her suitors and that can be as many as seven. They will follow her for as much as a month, and during that time the males may squabble amongst themselves. But once she selects one, the others do not interfere - quite gentlemanly. They merely move off in search of other estrous females.

After copulation, the newly mated pair establishes a territory and either construct their own den or clean out an abandoned marmot, skunk or badger earth hollow. The den is then lined with dried grasses or fur pulled from her belly and can consist of numerous entry points and tunnels branching out from the main lair. During her sixty-three-day pregnancy, the male will often hunt alone, but does bring food back for her.

The average litter size is six but can be as high as twelve pups, depending on where they live. In heavy coyote-populated regions the litter size will be smaller. If the density is fewer, then the litter size will be larger. It's all linked to food abundance.

Both parents participate in caring for the pups. While the female stays behind to nurse, the male will hunt for food and return with it. Until the pups' eyes open, which takes about ten days, she will remain in the den the entire time. During those days, and beyond, the male will fiercely protect his family against predators, and takes an active role in grooming and feeding his new family. The terrible down-side is, if the female goes missing before the pups are totally weaned, he will desert them. Interestingly, females that don't mate will occasionally assist their mothers or sisters with nurturing the pups. When fall arrives, the pups are old enough to hunt for themselves, and are ready to mate as early as twenty to twenty-two months.

Communication

Canis latran, means "barking dog." The coyote has been described as the most vocal of all North American wild mammals, with eleven varied vocalizations in its repertoire. These sounds fall under three types: - alarm and agonistic, greeting, and contact. Their most iconic sound is their high-pitched yip howl, which may deliver a lone coyote's message of being separated from its pack. This sound falls under the first type, along with huffs, growls, woofs, barks, bark howls and whines.

Huffs are high-intensity threat vocalizations. Growls are used in short-distance situations, but have also been heard among pups playing and copulating males. Woofs are used as low-level threats or alarms, and are usually heard near den sites, prompting the pups to immediately retreat into their burrows. Barks can be classed as both long-distance threat vocalizations and as alarm

CAMERA 1   10 JAN 2019 01:

BAKKEN

calls. Yelps are a sign of submission or of being startled, while high-frequency whines are delivered to indicate submission by a subordinate to a more dominant animal.

Type two is greeting. These vocalizations include low-frequency whines and group howls. Low-frequency whines are uttered by submissive animals and are often accompanied by tail wagging and muzzle nibbling. The group yip howl is emanated when two or more pack members reunite, and may be the final feat of a complex greeting ceremony.

Contact is the last type. The calls include lone howls and group howls, as well as the group yip howl, which is a response to lone howls, group howls or group yip howls.

Vocalizing is not the only means by which coyotes communicate. Body language is equally essential. An arched back and a lowered tail give a clear message of aggression. A bow, followed by side-to-side head bobs and a series of spins and dives is coyote play. A waving tail and an open jaw snarl means a fight is imminent between two adversaries, typically of the same sex. If they are males their stance is vertical, whereas females fight on all fours, causing more serious injuries, for they grip their challengers' throat, forelegs and shoulders.

Hybridization

Coyotes and dogs do mate, but it is rare in the wild, as their mating cycles differ, and coyotes for the most part are hostile toward dogs. But when they mate, and that tends to be in expanded regions where dogs are their only alternative, the offspring are called coydogs. The coydog population numbers run low for two major reasons: they mate and give birth in winter, making it much tougher for the pups to survive, and since the dog side of the hybrid lacks the pair-bonding trait, the female is left the arduous job of caring for the pups alone.

While the hybrids vary in appearance, normally they retain the coyote's adult dusky coat colour and, swarthy neonatal coat colour, the bushy tail with an active violet gland, and white facial markings. The violet gland is often referred to as "stud tail" - even though it occurs in both sexes. Either sex of the hybrid mirrors their coyote parent in terms of being timid and intrasexual aggressive -

same sexes fighting for breeding rights, male-to-male competition.

At Risk

According to the International Union for Conservation of Nature, coyote numbers are ever growing, even though the U.S. government has killed 500,000 of them since 1861and routinely continues to kill about 90,000 per year to protect livestock. Ranchers and farmers on both sides of the border, poison, trap and shoot coyotes. There is even an annual Coyote Hunt Tournament held in Alberta, offering a cash prize to the winning two-person hunting team that kills the most coyotes in one day. According to Lesley Sampson, of Coyote Watch Canada, "when we glorify killing at that level, where there are prizes for the largest coyote, the smallest coyote, the mangiest coyote - I mean, really, it leaves a bad taste in most people's mouths," she says. But conservation authorities state that the hunt will have little impact on the health of the coyote population. Perhaps, but aren't we setting a bad precedent when we endorse and encourage the mind-set of slaughtering an animal for the sake of a game?

Humans, as one might expect, are their prime enemy, with cougars and wolves running a close second. Unlike the wolf, whose public image has flipped to the positive side, the coyote remains steeped in the negative.

Disease is something else coyotes must contend with. They are believed to be the biggest carrier of parasites and disease among North American carnivores. Presumably this is due to their varied diet and wide distribution. The viral diseases known to infect coyotes are extensive: - canine distemper, rabies, infectious canine hepatitis, oral papillomatosis and four strains of equine encephalitis.

Something that is truly deadly for coyote pups is tularemia, a bacterial disease contracted through their lagomorph and rodent prey. Demodectic and sarcoptic mange are skin diseases caused by nasty parasitic mites that burrow through the skin, causing intense itching and irritation. The excessive scratching causes hair loss, scabs

CAMERA 1   28 DEC

BAKKEN

and lesions. Worms infest coyotes on a regular basis - tape, round and hook. In high-moisture regions, coyotes can carry up to 250 hookworms each. And by way of an infected ungulate, a specific type of tapeworm can enter a coyote and grow to lengths of 800-4000 mm.

In spite of all that is after them, coyotes maintain a strong hold on survival.

How to Stay Safe

Attacks on humans are uncommon and seldom cause serious injuries. Yet there seems to be a shift, with these attacks happening more frequently near suburban-wildland interfaces. As coyotes lose their fear of humans, they are becoming more brazen, chasing joggers and - bicyclists, confronting people out walking their dogs, and stalking small children. Intentional or unintentional feeding of coyotes is also contributing to their acts of aggression toward people. Don't let your guard down, even though they are a smaller predator and may appear tame. Any injury, mild or serious, is an indicator of how well we are co-existing with other species.

Did You Know?

Coyotes and badgers will assist each other in digging up rodent prey. Their unusual relationship could be construed as friendship, as a coyote has been seen licking the face of a badger and laying its head on it without any objection on the badger's part.

GRIZZLY BEAR

Grizzlies simply need no autumn accessory. Their profile is sufficient to get them noticed, as are their claws. A mere whisper of their name can evoke fear, and flood our psyche with images of an animal poised to rip apart and gut whatever is in its way. Hollywood invariably portrays the grizzly bear as enraged, with bone-crushing jaws, flared nostrils and sabre-sharp canines dripping with saliva, incapable of tolerance or tenderness. Myths and legends are built on this distorted image, but are guaranteed to form goosebumps when campfire tales are told. Add to our fright is the fact they move silently through the forest undetected.

We are terrified, but intrigued by the grizzly. Humanity's fickleness permits them to move through our forests, but not in abundant numbers, or so close that our paths are likely to cross.

If given a choice, the multitudes might prefer to see and learn about grizzlies on television or in the pages of a book, where they can safely unleash their adventurous side to share the domain of this fearsome carnivore. And that domain should not include their driveway, whereby the grizzly is heading toward their house, as this picture shows.

In 1918, biologist C. Hart Merriam listed eighty-six separate species and subspecies of *Ursus arctos*. And with that came a myriad of names:- Canada grizzly, flat-headed grizzly, Apache grizzly, barren ground grizzly, brown bear,

thick-set grizzly, plains grizzly, Kodiak bear, Alaskan brown bear, California grizzly and even a strange grizzly. Nowadays the list has shrunk to just one species and two subspecies: - *Ursus arctos middendorffi*, named after Russian biologist Alexander Theodor von Middendorff, and *Ursus arctos horribili*, which is Latin for "horrible northern bear." Quite apropos, some might say.

Habitat

Despite the fact grizzlies require a massive home range, and we humans have stolen most of that to support our population of 350 million on this continent alone, they manage to endure, and by all accounts stay clear of us. It's a marvel. Possibly one of the reasons they are still around is where they have chosen to live, or more accurately where we have pressured them into living.

Their knack for adapting to diverse habitats keeps them surviving even in the 21st century. They are not pigeon-holed into one dwelling region. They wander far and wide, often under the cover of darkness, from avalanche slopes that serve-up the occasional dead mountain goat, to burned-out forests with succulent new shoots and plump berries, to riverbeds and spawning salmon, to mountain ridges and abundant deadfall where ants colonize in rotting logs, to alpine meadows, where army cutworm moths congregate in crevices.

CAMERA 6   30 JUL 2019 05:59 pm

Each terrain offers some form of nutritional cuisine that incites this bruin to venture over the next hillside, down the deserted logging road, up the willow bank, through the mountain pass and now and again into the outskirts of our

towns. During these travels it may chance upon us homo-sapiens, and that's when life changes for both parties.

As the air turns crisp, your chances of meeting-up-with a bear increases. With exodus to their den only weeks away, they must prepare, and autumn springboards them into that preparedness. It is known as hyperphagia - excessive hunger. Bears forfeit sleep in order to forage for food, any food, to satisfy their mounting appetite - roughly 40,000 calories per day, equalling a weight gain of five to six pounds daily. Their metabolism drives them to consume maximum caloric intake. It puts them in gorge mode and on the move.

Hyperphagia was well underway when the following occurred. It was early that October morning when I set out to place a plaque on our two dogs' gravesites. As I approached our mini cemetery, I felt uneasy. A sixth-sense, you might say. Everything around the site was topsy-turvy. The wool blankets were unearthed and strewn in tatters atop the mounds. Patches of fur poked out from beneath the dirt, and their meticulously dug holes were empty. I froze. My eyes were the only thing that moved, and they were quick to spot it. That's when pure fear hit me. No more than eight feet away was an earth heap - some predator's

food cache. Everything I had ever read about them told me to get the hell out of there. I didn't want to take my eyes off the heap for fear that whatever was probably watching me might at any second crash through the bushes. I slowly stepped backwards. I prayed…"please don't let me fall, please don't let me fall." I knew if I tripped that would create the perfect scenario for a predator to view me as vulnerable prey. Every ounce of good sense told me not to run, yet every vein, every muscle, every fiber of my being screamed at me to do just that. As my eyes swivelled in all directions I wondered when the enraged animal would charge at me and how I was going to survive the attack.

Dale wasn't close-by, as he was off checking the other trail cameras. If a bear attacked I would be fighting for my life, as would the bear, for its food supply was its lifeline. A mere bluff charge wasn't likely to be my punishment.

Each reversed footstep put more distance between me and it. Whatever IT was? As is often recounted in emotionally charged situations, time seems to stand still. And I certainly felt that. Finally, I stood next to Dale, silent and pale. He looked up at me and joked, "Did you just see a ghost?" He soon realized that whatever had just happened was no laughing matter. Once we were safe inside our truck I told him what I had seen. We sat quietly and waited and watched. Several minutes passed, but nothing came barreling out of hiding. There wasn't the slightest movement in or around the bushes. No bluff charge. No charge at all. We figured our truck must have scared it away when we pulled up - probably not far away, but away from us human intruders.

Armed with a can of bear spray, I guarded Dale as he mounted a camera on a nearby tree next to the cache. At this point, we still weren't sure what species of animal we were dealing with. We presumed it was a black bear, or perhaps a cougar. Days later, when we reviewed the camera chip my mind dealt me a terrifying reality. Stories of gruesome grizzly attacks flashed through my head, and I realized just how close I had come to being a statistic. This big bruin had dug up and was eating our two dogs. We were stunned when we saw exactly what species we were dealing with, but at least now we would take every precaution when checking the camera in the coming days.

Like clockwork, the grizzly arrived near midnight and stayed until early dawn, - eating on and off, adding new leaf cover to his growing dirt castle, then resting his hefty head on his paws and napping, only to repeat the sequence all over again a short while later when he woke.

He returned to the graves several days in a row, until all that remained were the

BAKKEN

skulls and one paw. The coyotes arrived shortly thereafter, to drag those pieces away and salvage the remnants of rich marrow still lodged in the bone. We were rather stumped why the bear only dug up two pets when in fact we had one cat and two other dogs buried there as well. Was it because their scent was too old and couldn't be detected, with little flesh remaining on their skeletons? We'll never know.

Up until that day, there was no evidence grizzly bears existed in this location.

We had been told the only grizzlies in the area were in the Kispiox Valley and along the Skeena River. They were so wrong. No less than a month later, a beautiful blonde sow with her two cubs passed by our front porch. Clearly, we were living with grizzly bears, and we couldn't be happier. That was the prime reason we chose to move to this place, - supremely hopeful we would one day see one. And shazam! We did.

Initially, I was saddened by the idea of our dogs being eaten, but that quickly vanished when I thought how they had helped with a struggling species survival. We felt truly honoured to have such a magnificent creature make an appearance in our lives, to which they still do to this day.

Attacks

There are countless books packed with tales of fierce attacks by grizzly bears - sensational, graphic accounts of these sometimes fatal encounters. Newspapers sell when the headline reads "Hunter mauled by grizzly bear." The public can't seem to get enough of these tragic stories, and the following narrative is one of them. It is included not for shock value but to show there were victims on both sides.

It is the fall of 1983, deep in the backcountry of Waterton Lakes National Park, on a trail known as Crypt Lake trail. Trevor Janz and 24-year-old Patricia Van Tighem leave their home in Calgary to celebrate a long-awaited weekend together backpacking in the mountains.

Their hike is easy at first as they follow the switchbacks, then suddenly turns tough as the trail takes a drastic shift upward, leading them into heavy evergreen growth. They continue to climb, the trail narrowing and Patricia becoming unnerved because of the restrictive view. They pass a chattering clan of children, and some adults as the group trundles down the trail, leaving the couple alone again. Their hike presses heavily on their lungs as the rugged path continues to rise and the wind blows cold in their faces. Finally, they reach Crypt Lake, where they set up their tent, prepare supper then slip into their down sleeping bags and into a deep slumber. Morning greets them with a wintery wonderland: - snow blankets the hills and trails. They dress quickly to avoid heat loss and, after a quick breakfast of trail mix and frozen pita bread and

peanut butter, they take to the trail. Patricia is in the lead, feeling exhilarated by the beauty that surrounds them. Trevor doesn't allow her to stay in the lead for long as he whisks on by, calling her a "slowpoke." She nudges him playfully as he passes.

They cover the steep portion of the trail quickly then begin their decent. A bend in the trail and tree cover has Trevor disappear from Patricia's sight. Two steps forward and she sees it. A grizzly bear is charging toward Trevor. It's on top of him in seconds, its jaws clamped around his thigh. Patricia drops her pack to distract the bear and scrambles up a tree, believing she is safe there. But it climbs up after her and yanks her to the ground. She knows enough to play dead, not to fight. It plays with her head like a dog amusing itself with its ball - mouthing, slobbering and chomping. Then there is silence...footsteps...help... then safety.

Trevor's major injuries are localized to his face, as his pack, containing both his and Patricia's gear, protected his back, neck and the back of his head. His face is distorted when Patricia sees him later in the hospital. The one side is swollen and tight like a balloon, with Frankenstein stitches zigzagging over the surface. His jaw is wired shut, making it impossible to move his lips, which leaves his speech slurred. His nose is crooked and twisted, and his breathing is shallow and laboured, but over time he heals.

Patricia's injuries never heal. She will require years of painful reconstructive surgery, constant relapses in her recovery due to infection and permanent facial disfigurement because of one eye gone. Deep depression is her constant companion. When she can no longer keep the nightmare at bay, or subdue the demon pain, she takes her own life.

The bear that attacked them, unbeknown to them, had been feeding only 24 m (80 feet) away on a bighorn sheep carcass with her two yearling cubs. This is one of the most dangerous circumstances a person can come upon - a sow protecting her young and their food supply. The bear was deemed aggressive, but acting defensively. But that did not stay her execution. While the attack site was being investigated by the wardens, and Dr. Stephen Herrero, a renowned bear biologist, the bear family returned to the carcass. When the sow spotted the men, she charged the lead warden, Keith Brady. Although he shouted to deter her, she just kept coming. Keith raised his rifle to his shoulder, and as the bear lurched forward, showing no sign of veering off, or bluff-charging, he hit her in the kill zone: - the neck and shoulder region. Several more shots guaranteed her dead. Her cubs fled from the area.

Just what became of the cubs was never determined. They may have survived on their own, or more likely fell victim to predators, or died of starvation, unable to find adequate food to sustain them through the coming winter.

The following excerpt is taken directly from Dr. Herrero's writing, from his book, 'Bear Attack: - Their Causes and Avoidance.'

On September 18, 1983, a combination of circumstances - a dead bighorn sheep nearby a trail, the presence of cubs, and approaching hikers, led to attack and injury for the Janze`s and the death of the bear.

This was truly a sad tale. Even when the rules of travelling in bear country are strictly followed, as Trevor and Patricia did, things can still go terribly wrong. Yet there are far more encounters that end quite differently, with both man and beast as winners.

Winter Hibernation

Hibernation: "To pass the winter away in a deep sleep." What a wonderfully cozy, effortless way to get through those harsh, chilling months. However, to succeed and not perish during that time, the animal must be on its game from the moment it emerges from its den in spring to the time it dens again. That requires a great deal of effort.

The more I study fauna, the more I realize much still remains a mystery. For instance, do you ever wonder why some animals hibernate and others not? Researchers do their best to explain this paradox, and yet their clarification only leads to more questions. For instance, - the biographic and geographic facts that explain why a Richardson ground squirrel hibernates, don't seem to apply to an arboreal red squirrel, which doesn't hibernate in the true sense of the word.

The same holds true for grizzly bears. They are omnivores, - eating food from both plants and animals, and they do hibernate. But why, then, doesn't the fox, which also divides its diet between animal food and plant material? With man's highly evolved intellect, we lack the answers to many of nature's complexities. Yet we should never give-up searching for those answers.

As autumn edges closer to winter and bears have packed on essential extra pounds, they steer toward their chosen den site. Snug inside their winter home and in a curled-up position to retain heat and hydration, they stop all bodily functions. They don't eat, drink, defecate or urinate, and their heart rate drops from its summer rate of 63.7 beats per minute to 8.9. In addition their body core temperature goes from 38 degrees Celsius to 29 degrees Celsius. Even with all these physiological changes they are not considered true hibernators, for if disturbed they will wake up. And if you are the one who woke a bear be prepared to meet a mighty cantankerous beast.

The chosen den location, and availability of food factor into when the bear

actually dens, and that can begin as early as October or as late as mid-December. Regardless of when the bear retreats to the den, once it succumbs to winter sleep it will remain there, on average, until early April.

46

Spring and Reproduction

Once the bear emerges it remains in the den area for days, sometimes weeks. Since food is still scarce, and much of the land covered in snow, especially at the higher elevations where grizzlies tend to den, it eats very little and naps a lot, while waiting for its metabolism to kick into gear and return to normal speed.

As spring takes hold, the grizzly will venture to south-facing slopes and the banks of creeks and rivers at lower elevations. It is in these select spots that its nose homes in on glacier lily bulbs, sweetvetch roots and other starch-rich foods. The slightest breeze may also carry the alluring scent of carrion – avalanche-killed elk and bighorn sheep.

Just as Ivan Pavlov's dogs immediately began to salivate when he entered the room, anticipating a food reward, grizzlies may react similarly, recognizing the luscious treat of dead meat that awaits them.

When spring finally vanishes, to be replaced by summer's splendor of skunk cabbage, dandelion and mountain fireweed, romance is on their minds. In most localities, mating takes place in June.

The solitary male abandons his bachelor life and seeks out a female. Once the two are receptive to each other and coupling begins, it can last as long as forty-five minutes. It`s been reported that, midway through the session, females have sometimes lost interest, begun eating and even moseyed off, leaving the male trailing behind, still attached. Not a great boost to his macho persona.

Once complete, a process unique to bears takes place - delayed implantation. When the female is ready to den, her health dictates whether the three to five blastocysts that have floated around in her womb for months attaches to the uterine wall. In good body weight condition, two or three may implant. If she is in wretched condition, none will attach, thereby diverting all her resources to keeping herself alive during hibernation. In the case where implant does progress, the cubs will be born in late January. They weigh a mere 0.4 kg (1 pound) and are as small as 23 cm (9 inches). The ratio between the cubs and the mother bear's weight is astounding, at about 1/500 of hers. In humans, the baby weighs approximately 1/15 of its mother. The cubs are also blind and toothless, and only open their eyes at around twenty-one days.

Grizzly bear milk is rich, like moose milk. It averages 33 percent fat, 11 percent protein and about 10 percent carbohydrates, which equates to 41 to 88 kilocalories per ounce. In a day, the female could lose 4,000 kilocalories just nursing her cubs - the more cubs, the more kilocalories burned.

When the family finally emerges from the den, between April and June, the cubs typically weigh 2.3 - 2.7 kg (5 - 6 pounds). And two months later they may have gained ten times as much. They stick close to their mother for up to three years, returning with her to a den site two winters in a row, and emerging as a family once again.

The sow needs that much time to teach them all that is required to survive in a human-driven world: How to choose an adequate den? Where to find nutrient-rich foods month after month? How to stay out of harm's way - land development and people? How to successfully raise their own families so as to perpetuate the species?

Hunting

T is for trophy - a dirty word to many of us. British Columbia hunters alone kill between 200 and 400 grizzlies each year. They are the apple of the hunter's eye among trophy animals. And despite claims that only old and non-breeding males are taken, the opposite is the case. The eager hunter is gunning for the ace specimens, which are the ones that should be left to propagate the species. Evidence has shown that some trophy animals were in fact in their prime when shot. Killing the largest specimen in any species or subspecies eventually diminishes its size and survivability, as stated by wildlife specialists. Next is a relevant instance of that.

On Admiralty Island, in the Tongass National Forest, noted for its high concentration of salmon, intense pressure from bear hunters has completely altered the feeding behaviour of the male grizzlies. They are so wary of people they don't frequent the rivers to feed. Often, it's females and females with cubs

that tourists watch. For thousands of years, the males have come to these rivers to fish, but fear of man has reversed that. Bravo to the sport hunter for botching nature's balance, which matters not one iota to them.

There is an enormous outcry in B.C. against the grizzly hunt, with 96 percent of the population wanting it banned. Yet, until just recently our previous provincial government ignored the people's voice. Okay, so ignoring the people's voice isn't unusual for politicians, unless it's an election year, but what's bewildering is why our Liberal premier discounted the economic benefits of keeping grizzlies alive, what with the millions of eco-tour dollars they can generate. Even with the loud opposition, and the economic potential in eco-tours, it didn't seem enough to put a stop to this heinous sport. Constituents scratched their heads, wondering what else was needed to convince the government, and what else could be done to change our elected officials' decisions, since money and public polls didn't seem to be working. Electing a new NDP provincial government was the key to ending this.

Grizzly bear killing isn't just a matter of trophy hunting. For centuries, we have gunned them down for no other reason than they were there and we were afraid of them.

The plains grizzly is one subspecies we successfully erased. During a time of great abundance, when the plains harbored herds of thousands of bison and, countless antelope; when the horizon was darkened by legions of elk and enough rich vegetation to support all ungulates, the grizzly bear ambled among his prey with no worry about finding adequate flora or fauna. There were losses, sure, but there was also balance. Life was not teetering on the edge.

The introduction of strychnine and the repeating rifle in the early 1870s changed all that. The era of mass killing began, and the great herds of bison disappeared, as did the grizzly. By the late 1800s, the grizzly bear had been eradicated from the plains. Today, a few bears hang on in their former range - the eastern edge of Waterton-Glacier Park, Montana's Pine Butte Nature Preserve and the Blackfeet Reservation.

In northern B.C., we are fortunate to have a modest population of the mighty bear, and the proof lies in these photographs. Granted, they are not prize-winners, but they are magnificent in that they capture a superb predator travelling the moonlit trails in search of survival. Its glowing, amber eyes complete this ominous apparition.

BAKKEN

How to Stay Safe

Bears, by nature, are wary of people and show a great deal of tolerance toward us, even at times when we act irresponsible and reckless. Let's be smart when we are in their company, so they can continue to travel the wild country and so can we.

On occasion we're notified of a roadkill, to which we retrieve the animal and place it high-up on one of our trails. This young black bear was one of those fatalities. It caught the initial attention from a black bear boar, and then a grizzly, that immediately dragged it from the open, into the cover of the bushes. We were extremely careful when we retrieved the trail camera chip, and practiced our number one rule: first and foremost, be observant. Watch for signs of activity, including tree markings, over-turned logs, scat (fresh or otherwise), drag-marks and tracks.

Never get lost in thought or daydream, and for heaven's sake don't listen to your iPod when trekking through bear country. You need your senses clear and focused, and always carry a can of bear spray in either a hip or chest holster, not in a backpack that is difficult to get to. The spray must also not be a cheap knock-off, but the real thing that is EPA regulated, with a capsaicin concentration between 1 and 2 percent.

The best outcome, for the spray to be most effective, is to have the distance between you and the charging bear to be thirty to sixty feet. With that, spray a two-to-three-second burst toward the ground with a sweeping side-to-side motion, creating a cloud of mist for the bear to run into. Instinctually, you may want to aim for its face and eyes. Don't. You probably will miss and the mist could pass right over it. Several factors including wind, temperature and obstacles will play into the effectiveness of the bear spray. Nevertheless, having it with you makes you a wise hiker, prepared for the unexpected.

To increase your odds of not having to use the spray, ensure the bear is aware of your approach by making plenty of noise. You don't want to surprise it. If at all possible, have the wind at your back, so your smell gets to it before you do. If you spot a bear in the distance and it appears not to see you, then immediately return from where you came and leave the area. In all probability, though, it does know you are there, but you pose no threat at that distance, so it ignores you.

If the circumstance is such that you do startle a grizzly and it chooses a mere bluff charge to get its message across, don't try and out-muscle him by behaving as a threat. You will lose.

While camping, store your food and garbage properly, so the odors don't draw a bear to your camp. And when possible, travel in groups. There's safety in numbers.

One final recommendation is to stay clear of berry patches, salmon spawning beds and animal carcasses. Without a doubt this presents a problem, in that the first two spots offer favourite food items for both people and bears. So being there ups the odds of meeting.

Did You Know?

There is a Native American legend that says the beaver taught humankind how to build houses, the heron how to spear fish, and the coyote how to hunt. But before the bear could teach humans how to sleep through winter, a hunter killed one of them, and thereafter humans were condemned to suffer forever through the long, cold winter.

04:22PM 08/02/2019 0010

CHAPTER 3

WASTE-NOT-WINTER

Winter may seem like a season when the forest shuts its doors and hangs the "closed" sign. The air is eerily still, the trees are asleep, and the birds are few and far between, with the exception of croaking ravens, Steller's jays, Oregon juncos or black-capped chickadees, which liven up the woods with their flittering whirl and cheery chick-a-dee call. And if you have superior hearing, like foxes do, you'll home in on rodents scurrying beneath the thick blanket of snow. But aside from these subtle goings-on, the forest does appear dead. Yet, all is not as it seems. In fact, it's a clever deception that masks the hustle and bustle of winter's creatures. At times paths through the winter forest can be a highway of activity.

It is during this supposed sleepy season that a new challenge will present itself, and it will require all your super-sleuth skills if you are to witness the busy wildlife movement. The clues may be obvious or tricky rascals. Your talent for identification will be tested, depending on the freshness and depth of snow. If the snow is in mid-melt, that can expand and misshape the tracks, to the extent that squirrel tracks can be mistaken for bear tracks. Most important, don't contaminate the virginal tracks that stretch before you with dips and dives over the snowy terrain, or you will spoil the site.

The noise from your snowshoes seems to disrupt the serene silence of the wooded trail. You feel you should apologize for intruding on this sacred peace and quiet. But since nothing seems to be stirring - birds or mammals - your guilt subsides. You continue on, once again lost in your own solitude and drinking in nature's simple beauty, which surrounds you on this brisk, brilliant winter day. Then you spot it just ahead. Your heart beats faster. You are not alone, as you had thought. It emerged from beneath the spruce tree, straight into the centre of your trail - an animal track. A rush of excitement flows over you. What made the track, and where is it leading?

You drop your back-pack and move in. Your investigative skills kick in and you think to yourself, maybe the marathon of CSI shows you watched might just help you now. You think back to when someone had been in your office and you wanted to know who, but all that remained was the scent of their perfume, cologne, or BO. This time, instead of a fragrance, you have the animal's personal signature on the ground - at least until the weather changes and the ice crystals thaw.

As you look closer, you become confused. Is the track leading from the spruce, or toward it? It's hard to tell. You check for drag marks that would indicate the animal is moving forward, which leaves a distinctive line formed by the hind feet. Further examination tells you the animal did both. The snowshoe hare initially bounded en route to the trail, then switched direction and zig-zagged back to the protection of the underbrush. Why? A second set of tracks is the answer. A predator was after it. Its paw-print seems to come out of nowhere and suddenly mix with the hare's, smearing the perfect rabbit line as it takes chase. The life and death drama exited from the trail and continued somewhere beneath the snow-covered spruce boughs. Its conclusion couldn't be determined. You study the struggle you chanced upon. Did it happen just moments before you arrived, or during dawn's darkness? There is no way to tell, since fresh snow hadn't fallen for days? You leave the area and resume your excursion, but your feeling of peacefulness has switched to remorse: how dare you feel at peace when predators and prey are in a constant fight to stay alive? It jolts you into recognizing the reality that the forest is definitely not asleep. Once you review the camera chip the mystery is solved. Not just one

BAKKEN

predator was after the hare, but two. Was either one successful during their hunt? With no evidence of blood, I'd have to assume no.

The season of snow and polar temperatures is seldom considered a time of pleasure for wildlife. However, there are exceptions. Ravens and bears have been known to slide down snow hills, only to climb back up and do it again, using their furry or feathered bottoms as a toboggan. But generally, winter is no game to nature's fauna, but a trial of endurance. Some survive, others perish.

Humans are a different brute. We straddle our snowmobiles and rev the motor. We wax our cross-country skis. We snap on our snowshoes. We choose our favourite lure for ice fishing. We fill our bellies, don our thermal underwear, and zip up our down-filled jackets. We are prepped and hyped for our winter outing. It may be to some picturesque frozen lake, a snow-crusted meadow or white, powdery hillside. And when our play is over, we snuggle next to a warm fire, cradle a cup of hot cocoa, and replenish our depleted energy with a meal. But for the animals that are out in the midst of this draconian season, the scenario differs significantly.

Yet, there are times good fortune is bestowed upon them, and that was the case in the sleet-laden winter of 2015. A large ruminant died in the rugged Roche de Boule mountain range, and its carcass fed a whole cast of species. It was akin to a parade of stars showing up for the Oscar's gala: - wolverines, coyote, wolves, marten, fishers and ravens made their way to the frozen feast. Forgoing table manners, their only apparent nod to etiquette was that when each species' name was called, no other guest crashed the carcass scene. The dinner reservations were spread over separate days and times, but when they ate, they took their fill and then some. That's a given when there's no guarantee there will be a next meal. Nothing is left to waste.

WOLVERINE

Little is understood about the second largest mustelid - the wolverine (*Gulo gulo*), also dubbed skunk bear, hyena of the north, and glutton - owing no doubt to its voracious appetite.

To the masses, the wolverine is known only as a comic book superhero and movie character, but the real animal is as mysterious and mythical as the Himalayan Yeti, their haunts being similar, including snow-blinding mountains, which forges the mirage. To successfully snap photographs of one was like capturing a phantom, and a "badass" phantom, according to wildlife biologist Douglas H. Chadwick, who accurately stated, - "There's wild, and then there's wolverine. They may be the toughest animal in the world and come as close to mastering the mountains as any. And what an achievement it is for a wolverine to grow old."

Habitat

An article written in January 2014 by Niki Wilson was headlined "Humans are getting in the way of the Wolverine." You'd be hard-pressed to argue against such a headline, especially if you simply replace the word wolverine with that of any other animal the statement still holds true.

Wolverines are virtuoso adaptors. They must be, to exist across their circumpolar range, and overcome the barriers to survive we continue to erect; - excessive natural exploitation; -hydroelectric, gas, oil and mineral developments; - fragmented habitats; - human activities in once-remote areas; - transportation

Bushnell   03-19-2015 18:10:26

corridors, and raiding conflicts with reindeer and sheep husbandry, which in northern Scandinavia have led to the legal harvest and poaching of the wolverine. A mountain of obstacles has been mounted against them.

Dr. Jason Fisher's research found that, despite ideal habitat in landscapes between the Alberta prairies and the Rocky Mountains, wolverine numbers are higher in the more rugged regions of provincial and national parks. They don't seem to like being close to humans or our development, - "go figure!", so as people trek deeper into protected parks the wolverine is literally "running for the hills." It has been hypothesized that our presence and encroachment massively restricts the wolverine's daily patterns, so they avoid disturbed areas where their survival will be hampered.

There is still much for management strategists and conservationists to learn in order to make wise decisions that will allow this mammal to thrive in our human-crowded world. At present, in much of the wolverine's habitat, we are dealing with only very basic of information on the species' distribution and habitat requirements. Consequently their management is little more than administrative protection.

Their current population is unknown, principally because their home range can span over 240 square miles, and they roam it secretively. Are we the reason this species lives in these less-attractive, unforgiving environments? The answer is yes. But maybe the answer is not so cut and dried as that. Maybe they live where they live for reasons not yet understood. Although most of us will never have the awe-inspiring opportunity to see these rare hunters, just to know they are still out there helps to keep our wild places truly wild. Perhaps that should be sufficient?

The animals in these photographs came upon a carcass that was frozen solid, but they had no difficulty making a meal, or two or three, of it. They are noted for eating so ferociously it would appear they haven't eaten in days, or fear they may never get to eat again. There is a dreadful possibility that that's true, - as it is for most species in this century.

How these gulo discovered this remotely located dead animal is a wonder, but it does confirm their sharp sense of smell. Records indicate they are capable of smelling prey buried twenty feet beneath the snow.

These hyenas of the north stayed with the remains for several days. As the photos indicate, each wolverine was watchful while at the carcass, constantly eyeing the camera for any potential intruder. Neither animal was present when the other appeared. Although the sex of the animals was never determined, it is plausible they were a male and a female, as males will share their large domain with females. Yet current studies have also learned that kits will stay in their mother's territory well past the originally believed dispersal timeline, so these wolverines could be a mother and an offspring, or two offspring. Any one of those hypotheses could be true. There is so much more to learn about these mustelids. If they were more visible and perhaps cute – as, say, pandas or tiger kittens, the public's heart would demand they be protected and funds be allocated for further research.

Characteristics

If you were to pick just one word to describe the character of the wolverine, it would be dogged. That word capsulates other apt descriptives: tenacious, steadfast, unflagging, persistent and unshakable - these sum up what a wolverine is.

Their average weight is 8.2 - 19.1 kg (18 - 42 pounds). From head to tail tip, it is just 800 -1125 mm (31-½ - 44-¼ inches). And though their size may not seem so frightening, make no mistake. They are a force to be reckoned with - a typhoon with jaws and claws. Their long, sharp, hook-like claws function as a defensive weapon and are, - quintessential tools for tearing into a meal or, climbing icefalls, sheer cliffs and snowy peaks. The wolverine's poor vision is no problem for a nocturnal hunter, whose other senses excel, including an acute sense of smell and hearing.

Notice the distinctive long, dense, blondish-brown fur running along both sides and over the rump to the base of the tail, giving the animal the appearance of wearing a lavish cape. Their coats have made the animal a target in the past for use as trim and lining for parkas. Fortunately, trapping is less favoured these

days, as conservation-conscious consumers choose faux fur over real fur and the animal has been placed on the species protected list.

Wolverines have superior coats that provide prime insulation. It contains two different kinds of hair; the long, outer guard hairs that form the water-repellent surface, while the denser, shorter underfur traps a layer of air next to the body, keeping the animal warm. This hair combination is vital for the animal's survival in the frigid temperatures of its northern rugged range where it has managed to eke out a living.

A wolverine track is quite similar to that of a wolf, and can easily be mistaken if the print is not perfect, thereby hiding the fifth small toe and claw. Wolves have only four toes. When the wolverine steps, its paw spreads to roughly twice its size, turning its feet into virtual snowshoes, making it easier to walk on snow.

Behaviour

They are noted for their powerful jaws and stocky, bearlike appearance. As scavengers they are unrivalled in their ability to easily crunch down on winter-killed carrion, eating even the teeth and bones. Often they will bury portions of it to feed on later. They're highly adaptive, flip-flopping between scavenger and hunter - whatever is required to feed themselves. However, they largely depend on other predators such as wolves to kill their prey for them. These omnivores have shown how ferocious they are by driving bears and cougars from their kill, and have even been known to ward off a pack of wolves defending their fare. Not unlike a small dog running up and barking at a much bigger dog, - the wolverine doesn't consider its size, even when up against a larger animal.

One can easily guess why the wolverine also goes by the name of skunk bear. They secrete a gross-smelling yellow liquid from their anal scent glands, which serves three purposes. It is released as a territorial marker, - an announcement to females that the male is available, and as a defensive odor when being attacked, like a skunk.

Diet

They are not selective feeders, in that they will hunt and kill all forms of prey: ground squirrels, hare, mice, moose, deer, birds and their eggs. In one day they may travel 24 km (15 miles) in search of food, and still may not find any. Can you imagine taking part in a 25 km charity run and at the end not being able to stuff yourself with a large meal and beverage? That is the downfall of being a wolverine.

Whether the snow is powdery or crusted, their muscular legs and wide feet serve them well for chasing down their quarry. A reindeer can flee a wolverine in summer by outpacing it, but when winter hits, the tables are turned. In fact, the harsher the winter, the more it benefits the wolverine, for generally that equates to more winter-killed prey.

Reproduction

These solitary animals have an unusually long mating season, from April to September. The reason being this increases their odds of finding a mate, as the species is sparsely spread over a vast home range of 64 km (40 miles) to over 598 km (372 miles).

Wolverines are polygamous, which means a male will mate with several females. In human terms he is a definite player in the sex game - one, two and even three mates. But, unlike human players, the wolverine will mate with these same females for the rest of his life. Once they have mated, the female will go through what's called delayed implantation, similar to bears. The embryo won't attach to the uterus unless she is in good body condition by the time winter arrives. If she is healthy enough, she will proceed to dig a den, which in actuality is a snow cave that can be as deep as fifteen feet. Between February and mid-March, entombed beneath the snow in her surprisingly cozy wintery nursery, she will give birth to one or two white, furry kits.

New studies have shown that the old image of the male wolverine as a deadbeat dad is incorrect. The males in fact will visit their young after birth and continue regular visits until the kits are weaned at approximately three months. They also play babysitter while the female hunts. And once the kits are old enough to hunt, at six to seven months old, they will randomly travel with their father, but stay with their mother until they are full-fledged adults.

At Risk

One of the greatest threats to their survival is climate change - the warmer the weather, the less snowfall. Less snowfall means fewer covered areas and fewer burrowed dens the female is able to construct in order to give birth. That equates to fewer wolverines being born. However, 2018 proved a record-breaker for snowfall in the region our wolverine photos were taken, so as we continually shovelled we couldn't help but feel elated that these animals were given a brief boost to their survival.

According to researcher Robert Inman of the Wildlife Conservation Society, "better understanding how wolverines use the snow is crucial to understanding how climate change will affect the animals."

Other high-ranking risks to the wolverine include habitat disturbance, for example - snowmobiling, backcountry skiing and road construction, which open up the wild places to everybody. A British Columbia study found a negative correlation between wolverine presence and the presence of roads and areas where helicopter and backcountry skiing occur. Knowing this adds urgency to protecting natal denning habitat from human disturbance for this mustelid. As the supposed superior species, we are obligated to disallow pleasure-time hobbies from taking precedence over all species' lives. Having said that, I know they do, and without question will continue to be allowed, because there is money to be made in these leisure activities, and money speaks louder than a beating heart. I know I am naïve to think it could be different.

If it were not for dedicated individuals such as Rick Yates, Jeff Copeland, and several volunteers like Dan Savage and Douglas H. Chadwick, to name a few, who worked with the Glacier Wolverine Project for five years, we would still be at the elementary level of knowledge regarding these interesting mammals. That project yielded new insight into the needs of this species, and emphasized how essential wildlife corridors connecting existing habitat are, and not just for this species, but for all others that are locked into islands restricting their movement, hindering their genetic diversity and ultimately ending their survival. We must act today if we hope to give them a tomorrow.

How to Stay Safe

While the wolverine is considered one of Canada's most dangerous animals, having attacked humans as a direct result of being threatened or challenged, they generally stay clear of humans. That's wise for we are far more dangerous. If you encounter one, it will stand its ground. In that situation, make every effort to avoid using aggressive actions to scare it off. Its sharp teeth and claws and powerful body are no match for an unarmed human, and the situation could end in serious injury. Although bear spray has never been tested on wolverines, in all probability it would be just as effective as on grizzly bears, so always carry a can when out hiking. You never know what you might confront.

Did You Know?

Wolverines not only steal food, but mirror pack rats in the variety of items they steal. They raid hunting lodges and the plethora of items found within: knives, blankets, workshop tools, clothes, shiny kitchen utensils and other assorted trinkets they have no use for. The big question is: Why? No one knows. Perhaps they are the animal version of a hoarder.

PINE MARTEN

The pine marten, like the wolverine, is part of the mustelid family. It is often difficult to correctly distinguish them from weasels and mink, since they look quite similar, and all belong to the same family.

Habitat & Behaviour

Their distribution is far-ranging, preferring old coniferous and hardwood forest in northern hemispheres.

Martens are active all year round. To stay warm in the coldest part of winter, they burrow into the snow, which insulates them - a marten burrito. For food, they look for hollows in the snow around shrubs and tree stumps, where mice and small mammals may be. And the fur on the soles of their feet holds in the heat and serves as mini-snowshoes as they move about.

Characteristics

As nimble tree climbers, martens leap and zip from branch to branch, spending the bulk of their time hidden amongst tree boughs. The bushy tail helps with balance, while the brown fur with paler underparts and dark legs helps them blend into the foliage.

These shy, tiny animals weigh a mere 453 - 1360 grams (1 to 3 pounds) and are only 48 - 68 cm (19 to 27 inches) long, a third of that being the tail. Their soft, rounded ears, small, pointed face and willowy bodies make them quite adorable-looking, but that's a slight misconception for if you were to grab one,

ScoutGuard ● 2015.12.17 15:07:05

its needle-sharp teeth would turn this cutie into a handful of pain.

Diet

Since they spend the majority of their time in trees, martens prey upon chipmunks and squirrels, and will even pounce on their chosen meal from above. But when on the ground, they scour the forest floor for rodents, their preference being for red-backed voles. Honey, insects, amphibians, worms, eggs, conifer seeds and birds are also on the menu.

The marten in these photographs lucked out when it, too, came upon this frozen carcass. Although not the only visitor to that dinner table, it slipped in and out over a few days, taking its fill, - which, considering its size, probably didn't add up to much.

Reproduction

Pine martens are solitary and territorial. If they come across another marten they will show their teeth and growl. While neither sex will allow another marten of the same sex in their territory, a male will tolerate several females in his home range. The male defends a one to three square mile territory. Within an eight-to-ten-day excursion, it covers its entire range, hunting as it goes.

Trees offer martens prey and a safe haven, so it makes sense they would construct their nests in them. The female mates in the middle of summer, but doesn't give birth until eight months later -quite a long gestation period for a small animal, the reason being that it enables the babies to be born in spring, when food is plentiful and the weather warmer. She will only give birth once a year, to two to four kits. The young are blind and in complete need of their mother's help, but after six weeks their eyes open, and within three

months they are at full adult weight.

At Risk

Like most fur-bearing animals, their plush fur is a threat to their existence. During the 1700s to 1800s, they were trapped so extensively they faced extinction. Europeans loved the luxurious feel and the warmth of the marten's coat. Unfortunately, trapping still goes on today, and since there are no laws in place to prevent a decline in their numbers, they are at our mercy. Nonetheless, there is a glimmer of hope, and it comes in the form of the consumer's conscience -people's views on wearing fur have changed, so there is less demand for the pelt.

Humans remain the pine marten's biggest enemy, and today logging activities the prime culprit. Because martens depend on old-growth forests for food and shelter, clear-cutting destroys their home and leaves them starving to death.

Regularly on my way to work I am hit with sadness as another loaded-down logging truck passes me on the road. One more marten has just lost its home and its battle to stay alive no matter how much I want to believe otherwise. We live in a once heavily logged community. The industry has subsided somewhat but is still going on. Many people who live here earned and continue to earn their living through this industry. We are not among them. There is a marked difference between our views on logging and those of the locals. It is also fair to say my sorrow at a dead marten is not shared by the many of the neighbours.

The only areas where martens can hope to survive are those where the forests are inaccessible to loggers and their trucks. We must leave old-growth forests intact for all the species that rely on them.

04-01-2015 17:01:22

Did You Know?

Martens will stalk their prey much like a house cat does.

FISHER

The frozen carcass debuted yet a third mustelid: the fierce fisher (*Martes pennant*). So now we had all three "Musteliteers." The name is a bit of a misnomer, for they neither hunt nor eat fish; nor are they members of the feline family, and yet they are still known as the "fisher cat." Supposedly early American immigrants thought they resembled the European polecat, which was called a "fitchew," "fitch," or "fitchet."

Fishers are part of a large family, - the weasels, which include otters, badgers, sables, martens and minks. It's easy to see the likeness between them and martens. They are the big brother. Biologists call them middle predators, or mesopredators, - which means they are a notch below apex predators in the food chain. But they don't know that, for they can be as fierce as any top predator.

Habitat

Our human interference depletes other species' numbers continually, leaving history to repeat itself. And the fisher has been no different. During the 1700s and early 1800s, their numbers dropped near the extermination point because of uncontrolled fur trapping and the loss of forested habitat to unregulated logging and land clearing for farms. But toward the end of the 1800s, as farms were abandoned, the land rejuvenated itself and fisher numbers rebounded, as did the forests.

BAKKEN

Yet it wasn't until the 1950s that the fisher gained real popularity. Porcupines during that period were decimating seedlings planted by the timber companies to re-establish trees in logged-out areas. To halt this decimation, logging companies obtained permission from northern New England states to reintroduce the fisher, a proven killer of the porcupine. This reintroduction project was threefold: to restock the fisher as a valuable furbearing resource; to reintroduce a native species to its former range; and to utilize the fisher as a control device over increasing porcupine populations. The fisher helped save the seedlings and became enemy number one to the porcupine.

These solitary, secretive travellers prefer high, canopy cover in vast areas of dense, mature coniferous and deciduous forests. Some of these regions still exist across Canada and into the United States, but where they have disappeared, so has the fisher. They are fated to exist only in pockets of their former historical range. Thanks to reintroduction programs and protection their population now includes taiga habitats in Maine, Michigan, Minnesota, Montana, New York, Idaho, Vermont, West Virginia, Tennessee and northwestern California, southern Sierra Nevada and southwestern Oregon. Nowadays, like many species, they avoid open spaces because it exposes them, the predator, to becoming the prey.

Oddly enough, new studies have shown these adaptable mustelids have begun to move into open farmland, suburban backyards, and even semi-urban areas of the eastern states where they haven't lived for over 200 years. And they have done so because they've learned human development offers certain perks, such as roadkill, bountiful bird feeders, farmers' fields and well-groomed parks, all of which are enticing for unsuspecting squirrels and thus provide endless food possibilities for the fisher.

19°F ◔ 03/16/15 08:47 AM MYCAMERA

Scott LaPoint, a postdoctoral researcher at the Max Planck Institute for Ornithology, noted that one particular male fisher was even spotted prowling the streets of the Big Apple, - about which he commented that "the city's rats, squirrels and pigeons should be on high alert."

Fishers have shown how resilient they are, even when they are up against our amped-up logging practices. We chopped down much of their dense continuous forests, which forced them to adjust in order to survive, and they met the challenge. They are a great conservation story.

Characteristics

Their coat is distinct in that it lacks distinctive markings, and does not undergo colour changes with the seasons. They are dark brown to near black, from their tapered muzzle to their short legs to the tip of the long bushy tail, but with slightly blanched inner ears. What is unusual is that the female's fur is softer than the male's. Be that as it may, I wouldn't suggest embarking on a softness test. Besides their dense fur, they have five toes on each foot, with retractable claws, very cat-like. Perhaps that is the reason they are given the name "fisher cat."

From head to tail they are only 50 - 112 cm long, - the males ranging from 88 cm - 119 cm (35-47 inches), while the females are 76 cm – 93 cm (30-37 inches). Further to support the evidence of dimorphism between the sexes are their weights; males weigh roughly twice as much at about 5.4 kg (7-13 pounds) and females 1.8 kg (3-7 pounds).

Behaviour

There is no question these long-tailed carnivores are fearsome, for they mirror their cousin the wolverine in attitude and endurance as they travel many miles along mountain ridges in search of prey, but in the more agile, compact size of a ferret. Fishers can ignite into fiery, nimble predators and pursue prey that try to retreat to tight spaces; - rock crevices, hollow trees, burrows, logs, and even underground tunnels the prey devises beneath the winter snow. There's little escape when the fisher homes in on them. A quick bite to the back of the neck, and the chased animal becomes the fisher's next meal.

They are a quiet, shy animal, which makes them a poor display species in a zoo. That may explain why they aren't a sought-after acquisition for the facility. The now defunct Moose Jaw Zoo, in Saskatchewan, had one on exhibit in the mid-'90s. It was a one-of-this and one-of-that kind of zoo. As curators for the zoo, we saw the animal daily, or rather didn't see the animal, as he typically stayed hidden much of the day until feeding time. Fishers have proven even harder to breed in zoos. However, in 2008 the Minnesota Zoo had three fisher kittens born.

Diet/Hunting

What has set the fisher apart from other proficient predators is its Death Dance, with the wallflower as a partner. This promenade obviously requires two participants: - the fisher and the porcupine. Guess which one is the reluctant partner? The dance begins slowly as the fisher circles its prey, being careful to avoid contact with the 30,000 quills that stick in flesh like a blowgun's arrow - a wonderful suit of armour on the porcupine's back, tail and neck. To have its defences work, the porcupine must keep his back and fanned tail to the fisher at all times. Since the fisher is a low-to-the-ground animal, it is able to keep a close eye on the porcupine's face. When the porcupine makes the mistake of facing the fisher, it leaves its face vulnerable to an attack.

The fisher is lightning fast, and in a nanosecond hurtles forward and bites. The porcupine tries to turn away, but the fisher leaps over it to face-off once again with another bite to the face. Bite after bite to the porcupine's quill-less face weakens and disorients the animal, brings about massive blood loss and ultimately sends the prey into shock. This dance does not happen fast, but can go on for nearly an hour, with a dozen or more launched attacks inflicted. The porcupine reaches exhaustion, and more often than not is left scalped. By then the dance has ended, as the porcupine has bled to death. The fisher commences with the finale by flipping the dead porcupine onto its back and consuming it through its bare belly, neatly peeling back the skin while being careful to circumvent those wicked quills. All that remains once the fisher is done is a quilled hide and a few large bones. I never said it was a pretty waltz.

A considerable amount of time goes into killing a porcupine, but from the fisher's perspective it's worth it, as it provides several days of good feeding for the predator. When not hunting porcupine, fisher will make a meal out of snowshoe hare, reptiles, raccoon, squirrels, ground nesting birds, mice, even feral cats, dogs and small pets left outside - and of course, carrion, as the photographs confirm.

Reproduction

In keeping with the mustelid way of life, fishers only associate with others for the purpose of mating. The term of the breeding season is from late February through to April, with females being as young as one year old. The egg doesn't attach to the uterine wall for almost ten months, but once it does, the gestation period is roughly thirty days. Then, high up in the hollow of a tree, one to four blind, helpless kits are born. They remain with their mother only until the fall, and even before they are weaned they begin to catch their own prey. It is said their cries could pass for those of baby kittens. If you were to hear this in the wild, your heart might insist you go closer to save what you believe is a lost kitten. Let me warn against it.

Communication

Rarely seen, the fisher, along with its chilling cat scream, is often placed in the category of urban legend. People who are certain they've heard a fisher and recorded its call describe it variously as being like "a woman being attacked," "guttural," "a child being beaten," "horrific," "a screaming baby" and "I'm being murdered." One common thread that runs through these descriptions is that the sound is blood-curdling. Since the animal that uttered the cry was never seen, experts surmise what people were hearing was more likely a red fox or grey fox screaming, or a porcupine calling for a mate.

Fishers adopt an added form of communication through their anal glands. Both sexes have large anal scent glands that serve for territory marking or attracting a potential mate. When a mate is chosen, a cylindrical patch of hair on the central pad of their paws marks plantar glands that give off a specialized odor released during reproduction. It's akin to a man splashing on some cologne just prior to intimacy.

At Risk

Humans are again at the forefront of this animal's ruination. Climate change contributes to an increase in forest fires that wipe out older, cavity-bearing trees they use for denning. Highway hits and trapping for their highly prized, soft, lustrous fur account for the majority of fisher deaths. If you take us out of the equation, there are other risks at play: worms, tape, round and flat. Rabies and distemper have also been identified in fishers, but unless the animal is heavily infested or very young, or under other physiological stresses, the disease will usually remain asymptomatic. This is good news. With a parasitic and disease list as long as this, one might assume the animal can't be anything but unhealthy. The opposite is true. All of these seem to have had minimal effect on the species' health.

There is one primary enemy to the fisher other than us, and that is the bobcat. Not because it's preyed upon by this felid, but because they are rivals for the same food source, described as sharing the same niche. When your food source is depleted, so are your chances for staying alive.

How to Stay Safe

Generally fishers keep their distance from humans. As they expand their range to more urban areas they may discover that the space beneath your porch is a perfect den site, or take palate fancy to your itsie, bitsie, Poopsie. But other than those improbable events, you are fairly safe hiking wilderness trails and barbequing at your campsite.

Did You Know?

The fisher's hind paws can rotate nearly 180 degrees, which allows them to grasp limbs and descend a tree headfirst, giving them the potential advantage of attacking a porcupine from above, which makes the prey's line of defence of jamming its head against the tree trunk futile.

LYNX

The Canada lynx (*Lynx canadensis*) is a mid-sized carnivore. The word "lynx" stems from a Greek word meaning "to shine," - seemingly a reference to its reflective eyes. The lynx and bobcat are often misidentified, but knowing where they are found settles that confusion.

Habitat

This felid inhabits mountainous regions with old-growth forests with thick undercover, the perfect environment for their prized meal. Their distribution is vast - throughout much of Canada and Alaska as well as the northern-most states that border Canada, - whereas bobcats range over the lower forty-eight states and into Mexico. In regions where their distribution does cross, the bobcat is vulnerable to being preyed upon by the lynx.

Characteristics

The distinctive facial flared ruff that looks like a beard helps set the lynx apart from the bobcat. Its long ear tufts, which serve to boost its exceptional hearing, also characterize this felid. The stubby tail has a completely black tip and its legs differ in size, - the hind ones being longer, giving the impression the animal is bowing. They have highly sensitive whiskers, and their superb eyesight enables them to spot a rodent 250 feet away, the approximate measurement of 428 mice lined-up head to tail.

CAMERA 1   14 OCT 2018 04:27 pm

BAKKEN

Don't feel inept if you still have difficulty differentiating between the two animals. Several variables such as the age of the animal, the time of year or even the hour of the day could mar your ability to accurately name it. For the novice naturalist to be 100 percent certain, it would be beneficial if both animals stood side-by-side to clearly make the distinction. This is highly unlikely to ever occur, so just keep a keen eye and make note of all its features when you spot a felid.

Even though our photographed cat met all the lynx criteria, I still questioned whether it was one, knowing just how elusive these animals are. As their nickname suggests, they are "shadows of the forest" in their ability to blend into their environment, as the photograph shows.

Behaviour

These solitary animals travel and hunt alone. They are wary of people and other predators so much of their hunting is done at night. Since they are not fast runners, their hunting prowess is to keep on the move, - walk, flush, and chase prey. They will also use resting or hunting beds for prey to come close, and then they strike. A further technique is to sit high in a tree and leap down onto the unsuspecting animal.

Diet

Studies have revealed that the size of lynx populations directly correlates to the rise and fall of snowshoe hare numbers in their natural cycle. When there are bumper crop years of snowshoe hare, the lynx may consume up to 200 of them in a single year. In those same years, their reproduction rates also run

HCO ScoutGuard   12.09.2015 08:56:27

high. But when the hares are on the downward slide of their teeter-totter ten year phase, due to disease, then the lynx is drastically affected: contraceptive success plummets and the mortality rate in cubs rises to as high as 95 percent.

In the 1730s, it was the Hudson Bay Company, which traded in lynx pelts, that first noticed and recorded the recurring pattern of population fluctuation; it saw that skins were plentiful in some years and in short supply in others.

It is baffling, however, why the lynx doesn't merely switch to hunting other abundant prey when the hare population is scarce. And although they do feed on ptarmigan, small rodents, grouse, red squirrels and carrion, in some regions, they have evolved into eating nothing but snowshoe hare. This adaption puts into question how this serves their long-term survival? Just another wildlife mystery we simply don't understand.

There is little question the number of snowshoe hare affects lynx numbers, but what also plays into their numbers are coyotes. Both species prey on snowshoe

hare, but the coyote also preys on the lynx. In areas where coyotes are few, lynx appear more abundant, signifying that interactions with coyotes do affect lynx populations, perhaps even more than the availability of snowshoe hare.

Reproduction

It is only during the mating season that lynx will keep the company of other lynx, and that is in the dead of winter. Unlike other felids, their den is plain - beneath a tree stump, on a rock ledge, or tucked within thick bushes, making it easy to mistake it for a natural milieu. Only the presence of kittens gives it away as something much more.

The female will mate with only one male and is in estrus for just three to five days. If copulation is successful, she will give birth to an average of four kittens, sixty-three to seventy days later. The male takes no part in the rearing of the young, and returns to his lone life, leaving the female to nurse, nurture and teach her offspring for an entire year. She must prepare them for their life of solitude. During that year the solo lynx may be spotted travelling and hunting in a small group.

At Risk

For most furbearing species, the largest threat to their existence is - you guessed it, - humans. This certainly holds true for lynx, since their splendidly, long, thick coats are a favorite of trappers and in turn a favorite of the garment industry.

HCO ScoutGuard   10.25.2015 14:47:36

Essentially, their winter-insulated covering becomes a death sentence for them. However, things are again changing. CITES (Convention on International Trade in Endangered Species of Wild Fauna and Flora) governs trade in all lynx species; Canada, Eurasian, Iberian and Bobcat. Some of these are being reclassified - in Appendix I (in which every kind of trade is forbidden because they are most at risk of extinction), and in Appendix II (not currently threatened, but may become so if trade is not closely controlled to avoid impact on survival).

The IUCN (International Union for Conservation of Nature) lists the Canada lynx as Near Threatened, estimating the global population to be less than 50,000 breeding individuals.

The story is not new, but warrants repeating. Habitat loss is at the top of the list as an enemy to the lynx. Since boreal forests offer a treasure-trove of biodiversity, they seldom remain untouched. Road building, high traffic volume, urbanization, mining, oil drilling, and forest management practices that involve removing understory, which negatively affects the snowshoe hare, extreme logging and recreational activity all fragment, degrade and disrupt the lynx's home.

Consequently mortality comes at this felid from all four directions - predation, habitat loss, starvation and human-related causes. Their survival requires one strenuous struggle.

Did You Know?

A lynx can sound just like a beloved house cat. It purrs, hisses, growls and meows. If it were hidden in the bush, one might mistake it for a lost pet.

BAKKEN

SNOWSHOE HARE

The snowshoe hare (*Lepus americanus*) got its name from its sizeable hind feet and the marks its tail leaves, resembling that of a snowshoe. Its large, fur-covered soles prevent it from sinking into the snow and protect it from sub-zero temperatures.

Undoubtedly, this hare is well adapted for the northerly regions it occupies. Its shorter ears help conserve heat and its shifting coat colours camouflage it from predators. During the summer, its fur takes on earth tones, and once snow blankets the ground it blends into its habitat with its brilliant white coat. Only the black tufts of fur on the edge of its ears lend contrast to its ghostly appearance.

Behaviour

Snowshoe hare are crepuscular to nocturnal. As shy, secretive animals, they spend much of the day grooming, taking dust baths to rid their fur of fleas and lice, or they nap in shallow hollows, called forms. These forms are scraped out under clumps of ferns, brush thickets, and downed piles of timber. Low brush boughs provide hiding places, escape and thermal cover, which are vital for young hares. Heavy cover 10 feet (3 m) above ground protects them from raptors, and heavy cover 3.3 feet (1 m) tall protects them against terrestrial predators. Cover is intrinsic for their survival against everything that wants to hunt them. So when you remove their cover, they are doomed.

Diet

Primarily they feed on succulent grasses, ferns and leaves in summer, and twigs, bark from trees and buds from flowers and plants in winter. When carrion is available, they will take advantage of that, as well as stealing meat from baited traps.

Predators

Snowshoe hares have just about every predator after them, though lynx top a lengthy list that includes bobcats, fishers, martens, long-tailed weasels, mink, foxes, coyotes, domestic dogs and cats, wolves, mountain lions, great-horned owls, barred owls, spotted owls, red-tailed hawks, northern goshawks, golden eagles, bears, and even crows and ravens. Poor hare.

As a prey animal, at the bottom of the food chain, they must be alert every second of every minute. To assist with survival, they keep to the thick cover of brushy undergrowth. Their exceptional hearing and agility in darting in various directions and vertical leaps helps them zigzag out of harm's way. An adult hare can cover up to ten feet in a single bound and bolt away at a speed of

MOULTRIE ○ CAMERA 1 07 NOV 2018 04:37 pm

43 km/h (27 mph). But when fleeing is not an option, young hare in particular will "freeze" in the hopes they have blended into the background and become invisible to what is hunting them. When the above tactics don't work, they will take to swimming to avoid an attack. As excellent swimmers, they will even swim across small lakes and rivers to find safety on the other shore.

Reproduction

To offset the impact of predation, they have evolved into prolific breeders. Mating runs from January through August, with both sexes having multiple partners. The breeding season is driven by location, latitude, weather conditions and the phase of their population cycle.

The males will fight frequently throughout the mating season to obtain access to the females. They look like mini versions of kangaroos in the way they fight. Their powerful hind feet are used for kicking, while the front feet do the boxing.

Once the female's labor approaches, approximately thirty-seven days after conception, she retreats to her birthing plot - an area she has prepared with packed-down grasses. Her mood also changes and she becomes aggressive toward the male. Nestled safely in her grassy den, she will give birth to three to eight "leverets," and can have as many as four litters each year. In fact, a second litter can be conceived even before the first litter is born because she has twin uteri - a fascinating adaptation.

The newborns look like miniature replicas of their parents - completely furred, open-eyed and mobile, and within a month or less these babies can survive on their own. Unfortunately for 85 percent that means they won't live beyond one year.

Population Numbers Relationship

At their population peak the hare density can be as high as 500 to 600 per square kilometer, but can drop to zero in that same area during their crash. Outbreaks of disease are believed to be the reason. This up-and-down cycle averages once a decade with the period of bounty lasting for two to five years, then drops to scarce numbers and remain that way for years. These peaks do not occur concurrently in all areas, although in the northern latitudes the numbers do correspond a great deal.

For animals that rely on the snowshoe hare for sustenance, these cycles have devastating consequences, and that is notably true for the lynx.

The lynx and snowshoe hare relationship has elevated them to case study status; - they are now part of every biology student's curriculum worldwide - "the numbers of predators and their prey."

Bushnell Ⓜ 28 ℉- 2 ℃ ● 11 - 16 - 2015 15: 35: 03

Did You Know?

Hares will eat some of their own feces. Since much of the food digested is processed in the end portion of their gut, they must cycle it back through their digestive system a second time to retain all available nutrients from the food. Don't say YUCK - this is nature giving the animal a slight leg-up on survival.

CHAPTER 4

SPRINGS' SAFEGUARDS

Whether it comes in like a lion or a lamb matters little to nature's fauna. They live every day in ready mode. They are hyper-vigilant - always. They don't wake up and think, "Oh wow, today's pleasant weather means I can relax because spring is on her way. And there's the added bonus there won't be many hikers to run into because they're all at the malls for the winter blow-out sales."

Life surges and pulsates with the rising temperatures, and we humans are drawn to be outdoors. As we take to the forests, wetlands, lakes and mountain terrain, we feel revitalized, but it is also where we could potentially face injury or death, for we are not alone there.

All species you come in contact with share a mutual facet. If they are emerging from hibernation, they are famished and in immediate need of nutrients. Although still lethargic, they search for anything edible, then nap, then repeat the cycle over again until their metabolism kicks into high gear, which can drag out for days or weeks.

Species that have been active all winter are also ravenous, for surely food has been scarce during those rough months. Regardless of which category they fall under, both groups of fauna must try to quiet the hunger ogre before they can commence with the regime spring sets forth for each of them. Many times they fail and must carry on their regime hungry.

Newborns abound, and their care takes precedence over all else. Throughout the land, predator - prey showdowns ignite. Mothers of all sizes become fierce protectors of their young. They safeguard their offspring and are prepared to die doing so. The moose cow towers over her two-day-old calf as they travel the trails. The black bear sow has twice the workload, with two cubs to tend to. And so begins a new season.

MOOSE

Growing Up Moose

The moose cow faced the same diseases as the bull throughout the winter, but did so while pregnant. Back in the fall, she bred with a prime specimen of a bull, and as her calf grew inside her, for approximately 240 days, she eventually sought secure cover that would provide both food and availability of water for the birth site. Across all of their North American range, studies indicate, moose follow a notably similar birth schedule: - late May into early June.

This calf was born in late May, which should signify an adequate growth season ahead for this newborn. To survive, a calf must grow quickly. The birth timing is everything. If it is born too early and spring still doles out some cold snaps, it could easily freeze to death. If it is born too late, there is a real risk of inadequate weeks remaining for it to grow sufficient body mass necessary to ward off the impending polar weather of its first winter.

Moose mothers frequently nuzzle their calves, even well after giving birth. This helps build a strong maternal bond. As the youngster follows its mother throughout its first year, they are inseparable. The calf learns from her what it needs to stay alive in a predator-driven world and man's hunting season.

Unlike most other members of the deer family Cervidae; elk, whitetail and

mule deer - moose do not conceal their babies. When moose mothers move, their calves move with them. Cows will stand and defend their offspring, making them among the most dangerous and protective mothers, ranked right up there with grizzly bear sows. You'd be wise to be deathly afraid of them.

If these photographs had been taken with a person holding the camera; Tim Williams, a net gunner for Helicopter Wildlife Management, would say "all a mother moose wants to do is kill you." This was his quote when asked - what was the most dangerous species he'd encountered while capturing wildlife to radio-tag, draw blood samples and weigh?

Our trail camera did a perfect job, and with no casualties on the cow, calf or human side.

Characteristics

Even though these huge ruminants roam our forests, their retiring, calm demeanour should instil respect, not fear of them. For much of the year they are quite timid, and often when they inspect you it's with a curious look, as if they've never seen one of our kinds before, even with billions of us occupying this same space.

Spring also breeds bewilderment. Moose mothers turn on their yearlings. Their closeness throughout the prior year is now severed, leaving the young moose befuddled. It can't understand why she's acting aggressive toward it. The hair on the back of her neck is flared, and her ears pressed flat against her head. The young moose approaches

closer, only to be dealt an unmistakable threat posture by its mother. But still the youngster pushes it, and she delivers a quick kick, barely missing him. He jumps back and runs for cover. He is devastated. But why is she so angry toward him? And why won't she allow him near her? Dejected, he watches her leave, not permitted to follow. He lets out one last pitiful bellow, but to no avail. She abandons him.

Every May, similar scenes are enacted throughout moose country. "The desire of a yearling moose to maintain its relationship with its mother may be one of the most clearly displayed non-mating-related behaviors in nature," according to Bill Silliker, Jr. Our photographed calf wasn't dealt that fate, not yet anyway. It will come a year later.

The photos of the same calf were taken throughout the following months. It supports the data that a moose calf gains as much as two pounds per day in its first month and three to five pounds in the subsequent months. During this pivotal time, the calf will browse on leaves and twigs, but continues to suckle milk until weaned at roughly five months of age.

Moose milk is high in butterfat, at 10 percent, compared with cow's milk at only 5 percent. A Swedish company has taken this highly rich cream to affluent levels by producing the most expensive cheese in the world at $1,100 per kilogram (2.2 pounds). I think it's fair to say Kraft doesn't use it in their Mac & Cheese product. By late summer, a calf's coat changes from reddish brown to dark brown and the black circles around its eyes have faded. In addition, its once tiny, short nose has been replaced with a much longer version, a replica of its mother's. By the time fall arrives, the calf could weigh as much as several hundred pounds, as seen by the August 8 photograph.

How To Stay Safe

A fallen hardwood obstructs your view and the spring run-off coursing down the mountain creek muffles your footsteps. Neither of you see the other before the distance between you is dangerously close. The cow moose immediately goes into defensive mode to protect her baby. She holds her head high and faces you. Her ears drop flat on her head and the hair on her neck flares. If you take even one step closer, she will, without hesitation, kick with her foreleg and proceed to either chase you off, or stand and fight. In any habitat where moose are found, starting in late spring and going straight through the summer, you can expect a similar confrontation to play out. And although a close encounter with a moose can end in disaster, most often it does not.

The cow in the December and January images behaved much like this well into winter, even though her calf was on par with her size and weight by that time. She proved to be a fiercely protective mother. Potential run-ins prior to winter could have resulted in a bad outcome for this newborn if it got injured while running away from danger, or became separated from her, leaving it exposed to predators, of which there were umpteen on this stretch of trail.

This calf was one of the fortunate ones, for it made it through the vulnerable first months of life. Even with a powerful lifeguard as its mother, some offspring die from drowning, disease, malnutrition, accidents and predation. Some say these fatalities are nature taking its course - that is arguable. But what can't be disputed is the great loss for the cow, for future generations of moose, and to those who value a wilderness hike through a forest - a forest that demands your senses sharpen so as not to miss the secrets and wonders it holds within its depths.

GRAY WOLF

Wolves! Without them there'd be no "man's best friend," for they are the ancestors to every domestic dog breed, even the tiny teacup Chihuahua. I doubt Liam Neeson's blockbuster movie 'The Grey' would have drawn the crowds if the attacking pack had been Chihuahuas. Then again, I could be wrong. Smallish breeds do command your attention, inasmuch as their snappy, yappy behaviour can annoy. If you know wolf behaviour, you might take offense to the way the wolves were portrayed in that movie - cunning, ruthless, evil, blood thirsty beasts.

Of all the animals on this planet, the wolf (*Canis lupus*), has the longest lineage of hatred directed toward it. They were once considered vermin that needed total eradication. The history of their extermination came with vile, brutal, merciless acts delivered at the hands of humans. Ironic, isn't it? Our acts are reminiscent of how we depict wolves.

Characteristics

What comes to mind when you think of a wolf? It might be that of a masterful hunter. Perhaps it's their appearance, and how they resemble your dog. Or possibly it's their exquisite thick coats that made the fur-garment industry wealthy. Perhaps their sleek, powerful bodies, propelled by long legs designed

to run and chase down prey, is what you visualize. Any one of these notable traits might be conjured up when one thinks wolf. But, without its crowning feature, this species wouldn't be a perfect package, and that is their eyes.

The eyes possess an allure. They bid you pay heed. They bewitch and convey intelligence. One could deem them mythical in all they disclose. They are the finishing touch to a magnificent predator - nature's creation at its best. Without those eyes, one canine is an inferior substitute for the real thing. That is why dogs will always be the adolescent and the wolf the elder. Pay close attention to the photographs; - rarely does the animal take its eyes off the camera. It's as though it knows something is watching it.

Diet

Wolves are at the pinnacle of the food chain: superbly designed carnivores. They hunt to survive - nothing more. They are not senseless killers, as folklore would have us believe. In fact, though they have a unified tactic when hunting and show great skill and patience, only one in ten hunts ends in success. And those that perish at the jaws of the pack tend to be the weak, ill or aged, -leaving the healthy and strong to propagate. Unlike humans, whose targets are

BAKKEN

always the biggest and strongest with the prized-size antlers, whereby hunting ultimately weakens the gene pool.

Wolves will hunt the largest ungulate down to the tiniest rodent. If they are successful in taking down an elk or moose, an individual wolf will gorge, eating up to twenty pounds of meat in one meal. Wolves keep the ecosystem balanced, and without them things go awry.

One case in point is the well documented and highly acclaimed wolf reintroduction that took place in Yellowstone National Park beginning in January 1995. With the wolf eliminated from the park decades prior, the coyote population had exploded and the herds of elk, their numbers not kept in check, ate their way through massive stands of vegetation, stripping the banks of rivers and lakes of willows and important shade cover for fish and amphibians.

When we took stock of the damage done during the wolf's absence, the scientific world, amid a positive shift in public opinion, gave the green light to returning the wolf to its former range. Finally we could erase at least one black stain on our human history. There are few wildlife success stories that match the magnitude of the reintroduction, for it was truly momentous, and the public followed every step of its progress.

Decades later, Yellowstone resounds with wolf howls up and down its valleys - a glorious sound. For me, wolves Number 9 and Number 10 will forever be remembered as true Canadian royalty, - their bloodline extending back to the wilds of Hinton, Alberta. So, whenever I am fortunate to still see wolves in the wild I celebrate. They may not be Number 9 or 10, but they should be revered just as much, not systematically killed-off as enemy number one.

Regardless of the vital role wolves' play, allowing them to live or die is still a highly debated issue. That may never change. It falls to each person to decide the wolf's fate, or, as outlined in the following text, falls into the hands of the government to determine. Not a reassuring thought.

Hunter or Hunted

In 2015, the B.C. government hired biologists to radio-collar numerous wolves in the spring, not to relocate them, not to conduct some viable research on the species, but to easily locate the pack later in the winter, in order to shoot them from helicopters. Eighty-four were killed, and an additional 163 were killed in 2016, with more culls expected for the next three years – 1000 wolves, to be exact, at a cost to the taxpayer of roughly $2.2 million plus. The government's claim for the sanctioned wolf kill was that these predators were depleting our mountain caribou herd numbers. This is pure fabrication.

Habitat loss is once again at the front of the line as the reason our caribou numbers are being impacted, not the wolf. Nonetheless, the wolf is the scapegoat, as it always has been. Blaming the wolf offers an easy solution to something far more complicated - how to stop the spread of industrial development. Humans are like a speeding train with no one at the controls. In the meantime, let's just throw the wolf under the wheels until we can think of something else.

Have we not learned that when you reduce a top predator from the equation it messes things up? The killing of wolves as a remedy can actually backfire.

HCO ScoutGuard   06.15.2016 14:59:35

ScoutGuard   09.22.2015 10:29:57

Reducing their numbers can trigger a reproduction rate increase. And while moose and other game animals' numbers could increase, it comes down to one simple fact: the more game available, the more wolf packs are drawn to that region.

Reproduction

Pack dynamics can begin to transform as early as late autumn, as family members prepare for the onset of the breeding season in the dead of winter. Subordinates may try to displace one of the alphas, and if successful, allegiance amongst the members also shifts. But often the bond between the alpha pair is one of devotion, as well as both animals being in optimum health, so they rarely are pushed out of their leadership roles. In addition, they are attentive to preventing other members from trying to mate. Nevertheless, it does happen without the alpha pair's awareness.

During my years of working with a captive pack, I observed two omega wolves being relentlessly harassed by the others during this period - far more harassing than usual. Their attempt to fit in and rise in the pack hierarchy only exposed them to more aggressive, constant mobbing, often initiated by the beta wolf determined to keep them submissive.

As the harsh winter comes closer to its end, the alpha pair commences their courtship agenda. They do everything together - run, vocalize, nuzzle, lick, sniff and seductively play. Once mating has taken place, it's just a matter of waiting approximately sixty-three days for the pups to be born.

In years when prey is abundant, the litter size can be as large as a dozen; in food-scarce years, - as low as one. The den in which they are born can vary, from beneath deadfall, to a natural cave or a burrow. Even an abandoned grizzly bear den was once used, according to one biologist. Any location that provides the mother a safe, concealed spot is tailored for use.

It is during the two months following the births that the pack demonstrates how close and connected they are to the female and her pups, by providing her food regularly.

Pack Life

Food is the greatest determinant of the size of a pack. The more food available, the larger the pack it can support and the more powerful they become. During the first ten years of the Yellowstone project, several packs formed: Leopold, Chief Joseph, Nez Percé, Crystal Creek, Teton, Rose Creek and Swan Lake were some of them. But as time progressed, one pack began to fiercely claim Yellowstone as theirs and theirs alone, killing other wolves that dared challenge them. The Druid Peak pack made a name for themselves. They changed Yellowstone's wolf pack demographics.

Whether a lone wolf, or one that lives within a secure family, wolves exhibit a wide range of personalities, and no two are alike. Siblings, for instance, can not only vary in colour phase -grey or ebony, one can be confident and curious, while another shy and skittish.

That is what the pups born to a captive pack I worked with showed. The black female was extremely cautious, not venturing out of the den unless persuaded by her mother. The grey male was bold, inquisitive, and warmed up to his human caretakers immediately. Even with equal socializing by the keepers, the female pup remained aloof while the male took on the traits of a Type A personality.

There are several reasons why wolves may exist as loners. In the case of the omega, the wolf might leave to end continuous torment by pack members. It may be that a dominant member leaves to search out a mate of its own and begin a new pack. Or a pack member that has lost its status and is left living on the outskirts of the family could eventually choose a lone life.

The wolves seen on our cameras appeared to be lone wolves. They were never seen in the company of others, and howls were never heard. Without a doubt, these animals were aware of the other being in the area, as they invariably left some form of calling card. Granted, pack members do travel alone for periods of time, but eventually they come back together at some rendezvous site. It's all speculative as to whether these are truly lone wolves, or simply pack members out hunting on their own.

To us, it was irrelevant whether the individual was a lone or a pack wolf. They were travelling through our property and they were wild, not captive animals. What an amazing thrill.

Communication

Scent marking – is a silent form of telling others they are passing through, or staying to claim that fruit tree, that carcass, that harem, that berry patch. Most, if not all, mammals conduct this means of messaging. These pictures demonstrate a wolf coming upon an inviting scent and choosing to roll in it. No doubt he left behind a bulletin that indicated he was there, and perhaps suggested others stop, and enjoy the same sensation he experienced, smearing his body with whatever it was he smelled.

When I was a wolf keeper, I would offer the pack various items in order to stimulate them, and then observe their reaction. I'd drop clumps of llama fur, scoops of deer droppings, and sprinkle spices; cinnamon, allspice and nutmeg. Their reaction varied from extremely enthusiastic, to total disinterest. One spray however, that always got them up and rolling, was the fly repellent mist, which

MOULTRIE   CAMERA 6   09 JUN 2018 12:16 pm

was great because my objective was to rid their ears of snipe fly infestation.

Language – is the universal means of communicating. What quantifies as language is simple: - a system of sounds or symbols strung together to communicate a message. Humans and animals share the same formula when communicating. We use letters placed together to form a word, and one word put with another to form a sentence, either by speaking it or signing it.

Animals' communication is intricate, and we are still at the infant stage of understanding how and what is conveyed. Volume, variation in pitch and tone, the sequence of certain sounds and the duration of those sounds all dispatch something distinct. Whale sounds have been extensively studied, and so we have a somewhat better understanding of how these massive mammals speak to one another over vast bodies of water.

Wolf howls that are often mistaken for being alike are in reality quite individual. The limitations of the human ear are at fault for our confusion. We are incapable of differentiating that singular voice. It's as though wolves belong to a chic club in which, entry is restricted to those with specific knowledge of their language. And unless one has devoted years to studying wolves, as L. David Mech or Paul Paquet have, most howls do sound the same.

Wolves howl for many reasons. It is one way the family maintains its cohesion. They howl to communicate to other members where they are if they've become separated. Howls are heard to rally the family together prior to a hunt. When they return from a hunt, the members that await them howl with excitement. If pups are born, the entire pack celebrates with exuberant howls. Pups squeak out a meek howl as they try to imitate their parents and extended family. Howls echo over the land as the pack lays claim to their territory, as a warning to other packs to stay clear. And wolves howl for the sheer pleasure of hearing themselves - just as humans enjoy singing.

It often takes just one wolf to start the serenade before all the members join in. If a lone wolf is travelling through an already wolf-occupied region it usually doesn't howl. They stay silent to remain undetected. Something that is so innately wolf they must deny themselves.

Even though I spent years studying a captive pack, I never perfected my howl.

I could never get them to join in, or prevent them from looking perplexed as I tried to sound like them. They would nevertheless look over in my direction, or get up and come over, probably to get me to shut up, for it was painful to listen to. I suppose it was similar to a person singing off-key.

One particular male wolf at the facility, named Montana, loved to howl. One moment, he would be contently resting, then for no apparent reason lift his head, and while still lying down, let out a mournful howl. He did this often. I couldn't figure out why, or what he hoped to stir in the others. Normally, nothing came of it. The pack did not respond, yet he still seemed satisfied his single howl dispatched some communique that needed telling.

Wild Hybrids versus Domestic Hybrids

In man's quest to own a piece of the wild, we have turned our attention to breeding wolves with domestic dogs. It has become fashionable to own one of these crosses, and it has been estimated more than 600,000 exist. Because of their stable temperament, the breeds most often used for crosses are Alaskan malamutes, Eskimo dogs and Siberian huskies.

These wolf/dog crosses, no matter how fashionable, are controversial. Animal shelters won't adopt them out. They can't afford the law-suit if the animal turns aggressive and injures someone or some other animal. Hybrids have also been labelled unpredictable, eager to roam, somewhat fearful of people, and difficult to train. All these characteristics make them quite ill-suited for most homes. However, there are breeders who focus strictly on breeding and selling hybrids, because there is an ever-growing demand for them. Some pet owners are after the bragging rights to say they have a part-wolf at home. Others own one for the genuine pleasure this breed brings to their lives.

There is no right or wrong to owning one. The primary issue is to learn what the animals' needs are, both nutritionally and environmentally, so a quality life can be provided. If that is done, then the following scenario could be prevented. Reports come in on a wolf/dog running at large. It dug out of its fenced yard, or chewed through the leather rope it was chained up to. Now it is the community's problem. Animal control is called, and if caught the animal will be destroyed. If it lands on the shelter's doorstep, there will be the same outcome, for that is the policy. In either case, the animal will be euthanized unless the owner claims it and rectifies what brought about the animal's escape. Most times, the situation does not change and the scenario repeats itself and the animal's life is cut short - a doleful ending for any animal.

Just how these breeders can claim the dog is part wolf is an enigma. Does he own a pure wolf that he breeds? Or is it more likely a wolf from generations prior bred with some dog giving him his breeder animal – say, one-eighth? Perhaps it is the leg that is the one-eighth part. I am always left wanting to question the breeder about just what percentage of wolf is supposedly in this dog. Anyway, that is just my personal rant on hybrid breeders.

Years ago, as an SPCA employee, they brought a supposed wolf hybrid in for me to identify in order to determine its fate. That animal had no more wolf in it than what's in a typical border collie, and that's precisely what it looked like. I assured them the animal was fine to adopt out, and I felt certain it was not a hybrid, at least not a direct wolf-cross.

Wolf/coyote crosses – now, that's the real thing, and they are showing up across the eastern seaboard. They are highly adaptable and manage to stay below our radar, - rarely ever seen. These new predators are coywolf, or woyote, as they are informally termed - hybrids descended from coyotes. This new hybrid is one-quarter wolf DNA and two-thirds coyote DNA, with a little domestic dog thrown into the mix. These animals tend to be larger than coyotes and exhibit

ScoutGuard   06.29.2015 22:02:55

behaviours midway between coyotes and the wolf parent.

In 2013, the U.S. Department of Agriculture Wildlife Services conducted a breeding experiment. Gray wolves from British Columbia and western coyotes were the guinea pigs. Using artificial insemination, six hybrids were born. When measurements were taken shortly after their birth, the findings were as such: their weight, total lengths, head lengths, body lengths, hind foot lengths, shoulder circumferences and head circumference all indicated the coywolves were much larger and heavier than regular coyote pups. What was most fascinating was the 6 month-old pups' howls. Their howl began as a lusty vocalizing then transitioned into the high-pitched-yipping sound that is distinctive of coyotes.

Further observations noted these wolf-coyote hybrids form more unified social groups, and their play sessions are more amicable, with fewer injuries being inflicted on one another. Moreover, they reach sexual maturity much later than pure coyotes - not until the age of two. And what's most advantageous for this new predator is that the wolf gene gives the hybrid the ability to take down larger prey with its powerful wolf-like jaws, while the coyote gene gives it the element of adaptability, enabling it to live in human-crowded areas.

Since gray wolves from western Canada and the northwestern USA are not known to interbreed with coyotes in the wild, this experiment was undertaken to determine if the sperm of the larger western gray wolf would fertilize the egg cells of a western coyote, and it did. This supported the hypothesis that northwestern gray wolves, eastern wolves, red wolves, Mexican gray wolves and domestic dogs can hybridize with coyotes.

At present, however, the only coywolf that appears naturally, without man's manipulation, is in regions where red wolves and eastern wolves are found, and in southern regions where the smaller Mexican wolf resides.

Did You Know?

Wolves do not make good guard dogs because they are naturally afraid of the unfamiliar and will hide from visitors rather than bark at them. Clearly, this animal doesn't look very threatening. He picked up our scent off the camera, and came over to investigate.

RAVEN

The northern raven (*Corvus corax principalis*) is one of eight subspecies. They are among the smartest of all birds. They make complex decisions and display the ability to problem-solve. They can mimic the calls of other birds, and one special raven learned to copycat the word "nevermore." Scientists trying to present complicated problems for the birds often see them solved, which presses the scientists to come up with even more challenges for these corvids.

The Indigenous people of the Pacific Northwest regard the raven as a shrewd trickster. It can bring fire to people by stealing it from the sun, and it robs salmon, only to drop them in rivers throughout the world.

It is the subject of much folklore, mythology, literature and art, - possibly more so than any other fauna.

Habitat

The raven is found in almost every northern habitat: deciduous and coniferous forests, chaparral, mountains, desert, beaches, grasslands, islands, tundra, agricultural fields and even on ice-floes. The list would be shorter if I simply said where they are not found: in eastern forests and the open Great Plains. During the 19th and 20th century, when forests were decimated, the raven

disappeared from those regions. But, as the eastern North American forests regenerate, they are returning.

Behaviour

These large, dusky passerine birds, with their Roman beak, four-foot wing span and resonant croaking call, thrive among humans. They have accompanied us for centuries, soaring above our hunting parties, wagon trains, sleds and hiking trails, ever hopeful of a quick snack.

Invariably their clever, spirited, enterprising personalities, with their confident swagger, induce us to take a moment to observe them, for no doubt they will entertain. After all, if a group of ravens is referred to as a "rant," one could expect some in-house squabbling worth watching.

The raven's vocalization has been thoroughly studied by ornithologists - between fifteen and thirty different calls have been recorded. Of those calls, many were alarm calls, flight calls, chase calls, clicking and, bill snapping. Apparently a unique mate mimic call is used when one of the pair goes missing and the other imitates its partner's call to guide it back - quite extraordinary.

Currently, with their growing population numbers of approximately 3.6 million in Canada, they have become somewhat of a nuisance. They've been known to foul insulators on power lines, causing power outages. They tarnish satellite

dishes, pare radar-absorbent material off buildings, poke holes in airplane wings, steal player's golf balls, unzip campers' tents and rummage through open cars.

Diet

Because of their intelligence, they make dangerous predators. Often they work in pairs: one will distract an incubating adult seabird while the other swoops in to grab an egg or chick once it's exposed. With their expertise in raiding nests, they are considered a prime natural enemy to the highly endangered California condor. They also prey upon vulnerable species such as the desert tortoise, least terns and marbled murrelets.

As opportunistic feeders, during hunting season, the sound of a gunshot coaxes them to further investigate the potential carcass. They've associated that loud noise with a meal, - whereas other noises such as a slamming car door or air-horn offer up nothing, so they ignore it. So clever!

For the most part, ravens have a palate that will allow them to eat anything and everything they can get a-hold of, which is why landfills have such a heavy concentration of them. Besides garbage, these omnivores prey upon small mice and birds, all the way up to adult rock pigeons and nesting great blue heron fledglings. Even grasshoppers, scorpions, carrion beetles, maggots, fish, grains, berries, pet food and the primo tidbit, wolf scat, are on their grocery list, as is a bear carcass.

When ravens discover carrion, they must wait patiently to feed until the carcass is opened up by another predator, as their beaks are not designed to rip into tough hides. That is why the wolf and raven's symbiotic relationship works so well. The raven calls the wolf to the dead animal, and in turn the wolf will permit the raven to snatch some tidbits of rotting flesh for itself. They are sometimes known as "wolf-birds."

The ravens in these photos were fortunate because, a grizzly dug up the buried pet, and slit it wide open, which allowed them the luxury of helping themselves without the usual waiting period.

Reproduction

A mated pair of ravens will hold a territory and ward off any other raven from coming into their area in order to begin nest-building and reproduction. The bonded pair will stay together for life, generally in the same chosen nesting area.

The male will commence bringing three-foot-long sticks, wire and even bones to their nest site, which tends to be in a large tree or on a cliff. The sticks are then piled on the nest podium or jammed into a tree crotch, then woven into a basket. The female continues to tailor the nest to her liking, forming a cup bottom from smaller twigs, and then lines it with sheep's wool, bark strips, deer fur, grasses and occasionally trash. The elaborate nest takes approximately nine days to complete. It's not picture perfect, as the sides are often uneven, somewhat like a child's bed-making efforts, but it is substantially large - five feet across and two feet high, with the inner basket measuring nine to twelve inches across and five to six inches deep. Nonetheless, the soon- to-be parents are pleased with their nursery. These nests are utilized every year, but not necessarily by the same birds.

Between three to seven pale bluish-green, brown-blotched eggs are laid in late February. The female is the only one that incubates the eggs, and they take about eighteen to twenty-one days to hatch. The male does shelter the young by standing and crouching over them, but does no actual brooding. The young fledge at thirty-five to forty-two days, and that is when the male's duties magnify. He must find sufficient food to feed his new family. But luckily, he won't have to do it alone: the female will assist him with this industrious task, for even after fledging the young stay with their parents for an additional six months.

Camera Name0   59°F15°C   10-10-2014 12:28:44

The parents are quite proficient in protecting their babies by utilizing their large size, watchful-eye and cunning skills. They employ tactics such as dropping stones on predators that approach too close to the nest, and will even aggressively fly directly at the enemy and lunge with their large bills.

Bushnell Ⓜ Camera Name0   53°F11°C ◯   10-11-2014 11:50:57

At Risk/Predation

Adult ravens have few natural predators, but their eggs and fledglings have several: great horned owls, goshawks, bald eagles, red-tailed hawks, martens, lynx, coyotes and cougars. Ravens are survival-savvy, though, for they will wait until blue jays and crows appear at a carcass before they approach to eat, just in case there is a predator, or it's a bait-trap waiting to nab them.

We can only speculate as to how the rare white raven in British Columbia, with its leucistic blue eyes, is affected in its survival. Is its vision impaired? Does its lack of several types of pigmentation draw added pressure from predators? Is attracting a mate arduous and near improbable? Are ravens unduly stressed, thereby producing a hormone known as corticosterone, activated by the hypothalamic-pituitary-adrenal axis? Without the answers, we have no way to ascertain their at-risk level. But without question, these rare birds are faced with challenges no normal colour-phased raven has to meet.

Did You Know?

They are flying gymnasts doing somersaults and rolls in midair. One bird was spotted flying upside-down for more than a half-mile. And young birds are partial to the game of dropping ash.

PORCUPINE

The name "porcupine" is derived from porcus (pig) + spina (spine, quill). It is also known as the quill pig, for obvious reasons.

Porcupines (*Erethizon dorsatum*), are the third-largest rodent, behind the South American capybara and the North American beaver. They can weigh up to 18 kg (40 pounds), and reach lengths of 85 cm (33 inches). Their chunky bodies and short legs give them their dawdling, waddling demeanor - like a walking wind-up toy.

They are primarily nocturnal animals, so getting good photographs of them is difficult. Their preference is to rest in hollows of trees, or burrow under heavy bush cover during daylight hours.

Diet

These short-sighted rodents are strict herbivores. They eat herbs, twigs, leaves and green plants, but because they don't hibernate when winter arrives, they must switch to eating the inner bark of trees as well as catkins and willow, poplar and alder leaves. Whereas we humans have a sugar addiction, the porcupine has a salt addiction. They love it. They search for it by smell. To give them a boost, we placed salt blocks on the upper trails, knowing they would not be the only animal that might benefit. Several animals did take advantage of

this unexpected mineral supply, and took a lick.

Porcupines crave salt whereby they will gnaw on paint, doors, clothing, plywood, and even wooden tool handles that have absorbed human sweat. Their attraction is ill-fated, however. In their tireless search for salt, they are led straight into the face of traffic on those winter salted roads.

They are a gentle animal that chooses to scurry from danger in hopes of finding shelter. But when a predator prevents its escape, it will make a loud chattering noise, stomp its hind feet, beat its tail threateningly, hump its back, tuck its head between its shoulders, and the quills that normally lie flat snap to attention, to dissuade the predator from attacking. Like the snowshoe hare, porcupines have legions of predators after them - bears, mountain lions, bobcats, lynx, wolves, coyotes, eagles and dogs. Yet, it is the fisher that is the biggest threat, since it has perfected the art of flipping the porcupine onto its back to get to its legs and soft underbelly that has no quills, and can do this without getting injured.

Defences

It is the 30,000 quills, their prickly armour, that protect them from all that targets them. To the predator, porcupines seem like a very easy meal, - chubby and slow. But nature does a good job of providing every species with some form of protection or adaptation in order to survive. Porcupine quills are modified hairs coated with thick plates of keratin and embedded in the skin musculature. Quills are never projected like an arrow, as is often believed, but they do drop off when the animal tightens its muscles. When they get lodged in the attacker's skin, their body heat makes the backward-facing barbs swell, acting like a fish hook, making it even harder and more painful to pull out.

The guard hairs and quills are often used in the traditional Native American headdress "porky roach." In addition, the quills are dyed and, when combined with threads, used to decorate knife sheaths, leather bags and more. But most

recently, the quills have been found to serve the medical field. Their backward-facing barbs, when used as hypodermic needles, penetrate the skin and remain in place.

Because porcupines are remarkable climbers and swimmers, they have the wherewithal to use either mode to evade the jaws and claws of their attacker. Moreover, their gray or brown colour provides camouflage as the animal tucks itself in amongst the tree canopy, where it spends the majority of time - eating, sleeping and staying safe. It does this alone until the cool days of autumn arrive.

Reproduction

Autumn is when they abandon their solitary lives and seek out a mate. Loud vocalizing is heard throughout the forest as they attempt to draw an interested partner. Once a male finds a female, he will proceed with his serenading, but first he must switch his amorous vocalizing into a different sound that sends a message for other males to stay clear. If that message is ignored, the challenger will be dealt with mercilessly, for only the toughest male will have the honour of mating with the female.

Once dominance has been established and the defeated male departs, courtship begins. The winner will follow her around, grunting and humming. Then he commences to do a jig for her. I'm trying to envision his version of the Moon Walk. With his dance routine over, his repertoire becomes complete by urinating on her. They part ways immediately after mating, and seven months later - between March and May, in a rock mound, under a brush heap or beneath a log stump - she will give birth to a single, well-developed baby whose eyes are open and incisor teeth and molars are exposed.

A newborn's quills are soft and concealed in the hair, but within hours they harden and can be erected. And in as few as two days the baby is able to climb to escape predators. This fast growth cycle prepares the "porcupette" (as they are called) to be on its own when fall arrives.

Did You Know?

Although some label them pests, porcupines are extremely beneficial to our coniferous trees, for their favorite food is dwarf mistletoe, a parasitic seed plant of coniferous trees. This seed decreases tree growth, compromises wood quality and is a key cause of tree mortality. This charming animal keeps our forests healthy.

HCO ScoutGuard   06.24.2017 04:26:34

BAKKEN

CHAPTER 5

SUMMER'S SAVOIR-FAIRE

If asked, most people will say summer is their favourite season. The days are long, the weather superb and rainbow colours surround us in the birds, butterflies and flowers. And with these stimuli comes a mood change. Humans and wildlife alike mingle, romance and dote over. This is undoubtedly true for bears.

BLACK BEAR

Unlike the grizzly bear, that evokes fear, the black bear symbolizes a soft, cuddly and loveable animal. This may be due in part to President Theodore Roosevelt, who while on a hunting expedition in 1902 had a bear cornered and tied to a tree, but refused to kill it, believing it was unsportsmanlike. The news spread of his kindness and a stuffed toy named "teddy's bear" was made in his honour by candy shop owners Morris and Rose Michtom, - marking the birth of one of the most popular gifts for children and adults alike. And that's the rest of the story.

Fast forward to the present-day bear cub. Its mother is soft, cuddly and loveable toward her cubs. The collage of photos gathered over the summer months snapped intimate family moments and amorous couples. Love clearly was in the air.

Habitat

Today, black bears (*Ursus americanus*) are restricted to sparsely settled, forested sectors of North America, - a fraction of its historical range throughout the whole continent. Canada, however, can still act smug, for despite our annual bear hunts, poaching, and bears destroyed after conflicts with people, black bears still inhabit most of their original regions, from the northern tundra south to our U.S. neighbour, minus the southern farmlands of Alberta, Manitoba and Saskatchewan.

BAKKEN

The overall population was estimated at 396,000 to 476,000, as of a decade ago. But those numbers did not reflect bears in the Northwest Territories, Nova Scotia, New Brunswick or Saskatchewan. Bears have been extinct on Prince Edward Island since 1937. B.C. has a sound bear population with roughly 120,000 to 160,000, - about one bear for every seven square kilometres. This of course equates into more government-issued hunting licenses, 21,836 to be exact in 2015, making that year's spring bear hunt a record breaker, - up 52 percent from eight years prior. Wow, that's a considerable increase in revenue for the government to cash in on. I have difficulty finding the conservation aspect in all of that; - it seems to be more commerce than conservation.

Hunting pressures drive black bears to more remote, thick-understory terrain. The spruce-fir forest of the Pacific Northwest, with its dappled areas of meadows, river banks, avalanche shuts, roadsides, bogs, burns and subalpine ridgetops, serves up a vast selection of fare and the bear's preference for vegetative cover.

In less human-populated areas, black bears have taken to residing in less typical regions like the lowland, as well as parts of northeastern Canada, notably Labrador. The black bears there have converted solely to living in semi-open areas. These are more typical grizzly habitats, but since grizzly bears and polar bears are nonexistent in these areas, the black bear is safe to live out in the open.

Characteristics

A coat of many colours: - that is the black bear. Dark or light brown, cinnamon, blonde, silvery-blue and jet black, as well as the occasional albino, all exist among the fur colours of this species, with its light coloured muzzle and a bull's-eye white patch on the upper chest.

The texture of their fur can also vary: - wavy, sleek, sparse or shaggy. Their short, rounded, non-retractable claws perform as great tree-climbing tools. The soles of their feet are leathery and deeply furrowed, in dire need of moisturizing cream. Their ears are small, as is the tail, measuring only 12 cm (4.8 inches), completing the cute caricature image of a pudgy-bottomed, twitching-tailed, lumbering bear. But that lumbering bear can quickly morph into a 40-50 km/h (25-35 mph) running bear, uphill or down.

Black bears are highly dexterous, efficient in opening screw-top jars and door latches. Add to that their great physical strength, easily flipping rocks weighing 310 pounds with a single foreleg. Your Volkswagen Bug doesn't stand a chance if it's hiding food within its interior.

Behaviour

Black bears are typically territorial and unsociable, yet we have photos that show them to be quite sociable; – males mostly (adults & sub-adults mixing it up). They are seen mock fighting, eating together and walking the mountain paths as buddies. And of course there are the cubs that play with their siblings, and single cubs that use their mother as a play toy.

Bear's senses surpass ours. There is no question we are inferior to them in that regard. They have a superlative sense of smell, seven times greater than a dog's, their close-up vision is sharp, but distance vision is less reliable, so they trust their nose to identify the object. Time and again we have witnessed a bear, off in the distance, not recognize a bear it had befriended the day before, until the intruder was within striking distance. Hearing is their first line of defence, because it comes at them from all directions, whereas a scent requires the assistance of the wind. But if somehow they don't hear you coming, once the breeze shifts toward you they most certainly will smell you.

Be it land or water, bears are versatile - expert swimmers and runners. Seemingly they swim for the fun of it, but more often they are fishing for food. The day we watched from our boat, a young black bear swimming from one coastal island to another didn't appear to be finding it pleasurable whatsoever.

As he reached his intended destination, he had great difficulty climbing out of the water onto the cliff ledge, due to a badly injured left fore leg. It was distressing to watch from our boat as he struggled to get his footing and elude the barking dog just above his head, clearly bent on keeping

the bruin from getting onto its property. He moved awkwardly around the cliff side, his unusable arm dangling, most likely fractured. Desperately, he tried to find a spot that would get him to the top and away from the canid. This went on for a good half-hour - as we attempted to draw the dog to the opposite side of the property by hollering at him. The owner, hearing the commotion, came outside and grabbed hold of her pet. This allowed the exhausted and highly stressed bear to make it to the top of the cliff and bolt off into the bush.

I'm not certain the owner of the dog was pleased with our interfering, as she may have preferred not to have a bear close to her home. Nevertheless, the animal needed our assistance, and by all accounts was too exhausted to go back into the water and swim to an alternate island. It was never a question we would intervene, but even with that, the animal's future seemed dim with such a damaged limb that would compromise his climbing capability.

As a bear ages, its arboreal abilities lessen, just as we humans favour fewer stairs to climb as we get older. However, that is not a steadfast fact. We recently

witnessed a contradiction to that fact: - an eight-year-old mother bear chased her 18-month-old cub 25 feet up a tree, to deny it the food found at the base. As we watched, we were sure the cub would be safe, as she climbed high up into its canopy. But to our shock, that was not the case. The sow had a fixed determination to reach her daughter, and she did.

As the panicked youngster hugged the tree branch, her back leg dangled too close to her mother's jaws, and was severely bitten on her paw pad. The attack sent the tiny cub scrambling even higher, so high the flimsy branches barely held her weight, but that provided safety over her much heavier mother. The sow retreated back down onto the forest floor - satisfied she had sent a stern warning to her daughter, who she now viewed as an obstacle between her and her new breeding mate. The petrified cub stayed trapped in the tree for hours, and only when darkness set in, and her mother finally ambled off, did she feel it safe to climb down, and limp away, leaving a trail of blood-splatters behind.

I watched for the cub the days that followed, in hopes she was doing okay, and perhaps get a better look at her wound. After many long days waiting, she showed up, but limping quite significantly. I took photos of her injury, and was sure she would develop infection because of all the foreign matter that was gathering in the open cut.

There was nothing we could do, but hope she would heal. She did! It was incredible to see her walking normally within a short length of time, and her

paw showed no long-term defect. Nature's creatures are amazing. We were overjoyed with her recovery.

Depending on where the bear lives, near people or near brown bears, their activity level is reflective of that. They are extensively nocturnal when close to human development and die-hard daytime travellers when living among grizzly bears, to which our property supported.

Breeding

As seen by the photographs, we had bears pairing-up during the early summer weeks. At times they seemed to enjoy being together, while other times the female seemed to be setting the ground rules. An odd thing did occur between the cinnamon and black coloured pair; - they were still spending time together well into the fall.

In the midday-sun photo, that pair could easily be mistaken for a honeymooning human couple, the way they sat snuggled side-by-side, if it weren't for their furry backs. The pairing was not restricted to just female/male.

Bachelor & Bachelorette Buddies

Over the years we've documented numerous occasions where black bears choose to be in the presence of another bear. Those times seem to coincide when the food is plentiful, thereby granting the bears temporary relief from the

Camera Name   62°F16°C ○   08-02-201

HCO ScoutGuard   09.20.2017 17:35:16

117

BAKKEN

pressures of filling their stomachs, to engage in simple play.

Cubs

Who doesn't find bear cubs cute? They are a delight to watch as they go about their day. They can provide the onlooker with humorous moments, as they attempt to appear big and tough, or can wrench at your heart with their expressive eyes, and end it with a feeling of endearment when they solicit attention from their mothers.

Communication

Twenty different vocalizations in eight different contexts have been noted by author Gary Brown. Aggression can be conveyed with a growl, and yet recently it has been determined they don't threaten by growling, except in movies – for the audience's benefit. Snorts, bellows, woofs and roars can however, be part of their offensive. And, as these photographs demonstrate, ears pinned and charging forward, is this mother's serious message to the approaching bear that he is too close to her cub. She came away with minor cuts on her left side, an indication they fought. We had no good pictures of how the other bear fared.

Cubs will emit a "NumNumNum" sound, which signifies they don't want to share their food. Contentment comprises squeaks, pants, mumbles, and humming – a rhythmic pulsating sound a nursing cub makes, according to Benjamin Kilham, PhD, renowned bear researcher.

All of these previous sounds communicate to other bears and other species. Posturing and tree clawing/biting are other forms of getting their message out there. They are either disclosing dominance, submission, or a particular attitude. The higher up on the tree its marks appear, the higher up the bear is in the dominance competition.

Standing upright on its hind legs is merely the bear trying to get a better look, or a better sniff of its surroundings. Hikers often misinterpret this action as a sign of aggression.

The mother bear standing is a good example of her simply trying to get

CAMERA 1   06 AUG 2

CAMERA 1   18 AUG 2018 06

CAMERA 1   18 AUG 2018 06

CAMERA 1   28 MAY 201

09.16.2016 11:56:43

119

CAMERA 1   06 AUG 2018 06

2016.0

Bushnell   07-04-2015 09:04:42

HCO ScoutGuard   07.08.2015 17:23:33

BAKKEN

Bushnell
07-12-2017 12:07:2

Bushnell M Camera Name0 59°F15°C
07-01-2016

an idea of what she just smelled, or heard moving up the trail, in order to ascertain its' origin, and from that information decide whether to react or not.

The stance position is, from time to time, straightforward - the animal wants to reach an object that requires additional height.

Diet

They are omnivores, so their diet comprises both plant and animal material; - grasses, fruits, insects, herbs, small mammals and fish, - and as noted in the following story, large mammals. But, much of their intake seems to be plant base. Nevertheless, when a good supply of meat presents itself, they take advantage of the windfall.

It was early spring when we made the agonizing decision to put-down one of our old horses. Since the ground was still frozen, we were unable to bury him, so the other option was to drag him up the mountain trail, cover him with fir boughs, and let nature and her creatures continue the cycle of life.

Days went by with no feeding activity going on – it was strange. Then it occurred to us, nature needed some help. We cut through his hide, and opened up his cavity. This gave total accessibility to any and all creatures. That's all that was needed, to make the prized protein available. The animals that found this bounty were well-off, at a time when their natural food source was scarce.

Two sets of mothers and their cubs spent a great deal of time feasting, as did individual bears. The cubs showed no hesitation to dig right in, and dig in they did, plunging their heads deep inside the carcass. This food helped the black set of cubs get a jump on weight gain, since their mother was dominant over the

CAMERA 1   30 APR 2019 08:37

CAMERA 1   11 MAY 2019 04:17 pm

○ CAMERA 1 🌡 19°C 66°F   05 MAY 2019 01:00 PM

○ CAMERA 1 🌡 11°C 51°F   02 MAY 2019 09:15 PM

MOULTRIE ○   CAMERA 1   05 MAY 2019 12:20 pm

other sow, which allowed her offspring more time at the carcass to eat, and with less stress than the cinnamon and black coloured cubs.

A series of photos show the black sow periodically wandering off, leaving her cubs behind, but she was never gone for long. Yet, it was evidence of things to come – a month later she would abandon them permanently.

The bears returned to feed over several days, and only when a large, dominate male entered the scene did they leave the protein larder. When the big bruin left, golden eagles landed and took their turn. Even a wary lone wolf made an appearance, but was too nervous to eat, so didn't stay for more than a few minutes.

Eventually, something dragged the carcass deep into the woods leaving behind only remnants of a tail, some mane hair and flies – hordes of flies that latched onto whatever animal stopped by. We stopped by, but because we didn't rummage around the bits and pieces that were left we were spared the annoyance of insects, and came away only with wonderful memories of our horse, and how in death he aided the survival of other creatures.

Did You Know?

A wolf growl is often used in movies as a bear sound, because people have come to believe that is the vocalization of an angry bear. For the most part growls are absent from a bear's range of sounds.

BAKKEN

MULE DEER

Mule deer (*Odocoileus hemionus*) or burro deer get their name from their overly large ears that move independently and constantly, like a satellite dish bouncing sounds off them. I would think as our world gets noisier and sound pollution increases, these deer must suffer greatly with no means to quiet things down. In our region, with its train horns, ambulance and police sirens, low-flying helicopters and barking dogs, their ears are kept perked at most times. I hope they have become desensitized and able to ignore these recurring noises, otherwise they'd burn excessive energy being constantly on the alert.

Habitat

Their numbers are often small, wherever they are found, for their herd size most often consists only of a doe and her fawn or fawns, and a pair of yearlings. At varying seasons they inhabit every sort of ecological zone, from valley bottoms to alpine. Forest edges, mountains and foothills are their home most months, and it was at the base of a mountain where our trail camera caught pictures of them.

HCO ScoutGuard   07.27.2014 11:13:27

Rarely do they stray far from the tree line. Farmed fields, however, have such an allure it draws them out into the open, where they become extremely vulnerable, particularly during hunting season.

It is estimated that 20,000 to 25,000 occupy the northern ranges of British Columbia. To ensure there is food and cover for all, the family groups space themselves far apart. If does encounter one another they will fight, protecting their little geographic corner.

Diet

They are either considered a nuisance when they raid your garden, or a pleasant reminder of your Bambi years growing up. If they are in your garden, chances are they are after your apples, strawberries, assortment of greens and everything in between. A study conducted in 1973 found 788 species of plants were eaten by mule deer. Clearly, herbaceous plants make up the major part of their summer diet, along with huckleberry, salal, thimbleberry and blackberry. Come winter they browse on buds and twigs of Douglas fir, cedar, yew, aspen, willow dogwood, serviceberry, juniper and sage.

Like all ungulates they face the same situation - competition with free-grazing cattle. The more cattle required to fill our bellies, the less vegetation for nature's wildlife to feed on.

Characteristics

Their fur changes with the seasons. In summer, they are a tan or reddish-brown, almost copper colour; - certainly, the fawns are. Winter has them toned down to a grayish-brown, duplicating the dull gray sky days.

Their tail droops, not uplifted like the whitetail deer, but it does communicate danger to others in the herd and provide a beacon for the fawn to follow during flight. The mule deer's white patches are found on the rump, inside the ears, under the throat, and the inner side of the legs. So as they bound (pronking, or stotting), as it is known when all four feet come down together through the forest you would see flashes of white as they reach a speed of 72 km/h (45 mph).

But it is their antlers that set them apart from whitetail. Their configuration is quite different. They fork as they grow, rather than branching from a single main beam. Each antler has a separate beam that forks into two tines (dichotomous branching), and can spread to 120 cm (4 feet). The duo tines are clearly seen in the photographs, and the antlers are well developed by early summer, for they begin to regrow almost immediately after shedding the old ones in mid-February.

Behaviour

In the Pacific Northwest, where there are mountain ranges, the deer migrate up and down through the changing seasons to bypass heavy snows, as it is strenuous for them to manoeuvre through snow deeper than 30 cm.

If you are observant, they leave calling cards. Their droppings are easy to identify, but it takes a keen eye to spot buck rubs, browse marks, scrapings and beds. An even keener eye can determine the sex of the animal from its resting bed. When they stand, both sexes will urinate, the doe off to one side, while the buck urinates directly in the middle of it.

Reproduction

All ungulates engage in the autumn rut. One major difference between mule deer bucks and moose is that they do control their females and form harems. Their antlers follow the same growth cycle as the moose. Bucks for the most part are solitary, but some band together before and after the rut. To keep their females from wandering off, or being wooed by another, the buck constantly guards them. Exhaustion from policing his harem or fighting challengers is part of what they must endure. To alleviate some of this energy output, the buck will commence with circling a rival using deliberate steps, head low, back arched, tail flicking and front hooves flailing. Most times this is sufficient to stave off any further conflict.

However, when this is not resolved, the males' face-off and vigorous fights ensue. Each animal tries to force the other's head down, and doing so often results in their antlers becoming enmeshed. They violently struggle to overpower the other, which either frees them from their padlocked plight, or guarantees both will eventually succumb to starvation.

The bucks that don't become entangled also suffer. The prolonged rut, with its apex of activity, leaves them feeble, with wounds, broken antlers and lost weight, all of this with scarcely time to recover before winter hits. Some will be killed by predators, while others die of malnutrition, as they are too weak to combat winter's harshness. The price tag for propagating is huge.

Despite the hardships they must face to reproduce, they manage to be fruitful and can double their population in just a few years if the conditions are suitable. The hunter harvest, starvation, predation and a high fawn mortality rate of 45 to 70 percent requires this species to be prolific if they are to maintain a hold on survival.

Communication

With the aid of pheromones or scents that come from several glands, they are able to deliver the desired message. The following three glands are the major communicators. The metatarsal (outside of lower leg) produces an alarm scent. The tarsal (inside of hock) signals mutual recognition. The interdigital (between the toes) deposits a scent trail as they travel.

At Risk

Every year, several thousand mule deer die on British Columbia highways and roads alone. To that toll add heavy livestock grazing, which has detrimental effects on the deer's winter-spring range. Add the deer's value to recreational hunters, who kill approximately 20,000 of them annually. And then add the final dollop to the list of culprits: habitat loss. Deer-habitat continues to disappear as our population increases and we ravage the land with our residential development, hydroelectric reservoirs, surface mining, agricultural land development and highways. We humans have succeeded at putting severe survival pressure on these ungulates.

Did You Know?

It's ironic how some exploits and disasters annihilate many species, yet benefit others. This holds true in the case of mule deer. Logging and forest fires actually aid them, increasing openings where new vegetation can take hold and become abundant, thereby increasing deer numbers.

CHAPTER 6

EVERY ANIMAL HAS ITS DAY

The yearly calendar is crammed with wacky, divine, virtuous, relevant and historic days that are celebrated month after month. I'll cite some that commemorate wildlife. When these dates roll around, stop and take a moment to ask yourself if you can do more to help them along.

January

5th - "National Bird Day": This is a day that should be celebrated every day, in view of the fact we see fewer and fewer flocks of song-birds, parrots and seabirds darkening our skies that once was the case. Without birds, our ears would be robbed of enchanting music and our eyes of flying rainbows. We also may never have been inspired to build machines that allowed us to view our world from the air. We owe birds much.

16th -"Appreciate a Dragon Day": Off the top one might think this was a fantasy-based day. But you'd be wrong, for dragons live among us here and now. There is the ever-popular pet-store lizard, the bearded dragon, - the iridescent dragonfly, and the primordial-looking Komodo dragon. Fantasy is often drawn from real life.

21st -"Squirrel Appreciation Day": Without these and other small prey animals, terrestrial and aerial predators would be hard-pressed to find adequate food, since *Sciuridae* (rodents) often are an important supplement to their overall diet, even for the mighty grizzly bear. So the next time a squirrel scurries across your yard, let it jog your memory of its importance in nature's food chain.

February

2nd -"Groundhog Day": If we didn't acknowledge this event, are we to assume we mere mortals wouldn't know when spring was coming and winter was ending. If that is the case, then thank goodness for the noble groundhog.

20th -"Love Your Pet Day": With millions of pet owners throughout the world, who already love their pets dearly, you don't need a specific day to celebrate that fact. I believe this day is a reminder to the small percentage of pet owners who need to do a better job providing a quality life for their animal - more affection, more food, water, shelter, security and, when possible, a home away from the raw elements. Your pet will show you unconditional love and devotion in return.

27th -"Polar Bear Day": With melting glaciers, and devastating changes to weather patterns, global warming (the guilty party) has risen to the top of the Most Wanted list, driven by our own fossil fuels. These have brought the iconic polar bear to a ruinous situation. They rely completely on ice to hunt for seals. Without ice, they can't sneak up on these marine mammals and obtain a meal. Studies show that the sea ice is forming later and later each year. The bears already go months without eating. Let's not bring them to outright starvation before taking action. We must not lose these magnificent carnivores, because polar bears are synonymous with Canada. They are but one example of what makes Canada great.

March

14th -"Learn about Butterflies Day": These delicate, luminous creatures brighten even the darkest days. Make a point to learn just one thing about these colourful fairies, and marvel once again at the astonishing migratory journey the monarch butterfly undertakes every year.

20th -"International Earth Day": This date should have a permanent place at the podium. The multitude of events that take place on the first day of spring show the spirit of people toward this great planet - so, kudos to those who step-up in the name of preserving Mother Earth. Let's not eradicate one more species before we have even discovered it.

21ˢᵗ -"Fragrance Day": My impression of what this day is has nothing to do with a spritz of anything from a bottle. The gist is to revel in the fragrance of freshly cut grass, an ocean breeze, petrichor (the smell of the air after a rainstorm), a bonanza of smells wafting from a field of wild flowers, the heavy musk odor from a rutting ungulate, the defensive spray from a skunk or the pungent aroma of a forest floor.

April

4ᵗʰ -"World Rat Day": Definitely we should pay homage to these rodents, for they have given their minds and bodies in the name of medical and scientific research. They have had electrodes attached to their heads, toxins laced into their food, been injected with who knows what liquid and fed huge levels of saccharin which brought about bladder cancer, all for the purpose of determining the health risks to humans. So the next time you want to say yuck to these long-bare-naked tailed animals you should instead shout out a big THANK YOU.

8ᵗʰ -"Zoo Lover's Day": As previous zoo employees of twenty plus years, we simply want to say: enjoy, learn, cherish, revere and be awed by what else lives on this planet with us, for without these kinds of facilities much of mankind would be deprived of seeing the splendor and wonders of wildlife.

17ᵗʰ -"Bat Appreciation Day": The giant fruit, vampire, little brown, hog-nosed, Honduran white or bumblebee bat (the latter weighing only 2 grams, making it the smallest mammal in the world), come in varying sizes ranging to as large as a small dog. There are over 1,100 identified species, all of which deserve guardianship, for in addition to cross-fertilizing they provide a service of controlling insect numbers by consuming huge volumes of them, making them a protector to the agriculture industry. We need to think of bats in a more positive light, rather than being afraid of them as possible carriers of rabies. On this Bat Appreciation Day, build a bat house, maintain habitat that has clear, open water, and grow hedge-rows for them to fly between, which provide protection from owls. They are one of man's best friends, even if we don't realize it.

25ᵗʰ -"World Penguin Day": You can count on getting a laugh if you dress in a tuxedo and waddle around mimicking a penguin. However, aside from providing some comic relief, they deserve our admiration for being pillars of stamina - just watch 'March of the Penguins.' You will have a new-found respect for the herculean task they undertake to care for their unhatched egg. No matter the species of penguin - emperor, Adelie, rockhopper, gentoo, crested, chinstrap, macaroni or king, the mated pair will experience either great joy when the baby hatches or heartbreak when it doesn't. Depending on where they live, it may have frozen to death on the Antarctic ice sheet with temperatures plunging to -50 Celsius, and wind gusts rising to 200 km per hour.

May

1st -"Save the Rhino Day": As is true for the elephant, poachers are armed and ready to do whatever it takes to get that rhino horn, which is worth a lot of money on the black market. Certain compounds found within the horn are extracted to create some bizarre concoction that will allegedly heal what ails you: gout, fever, rheumatism, snakebites, hallucinations, carbuncles, and my favourite - devil possession. Recently in the news a person broke into a zoo and killed a captive rhino, then hacked off his horn. A pretty brazen act, but to the perpetrator, clearly the monetary gain outweighed the risks. Zoos are being proactive and cutting off their rhino's horns, which can be done without harming the animal, and thereby eliminating this prized body part. Unfortunately, this does nothing to help the wild population that are killed to make this powered or liquid brew. The last male northern white rhino died in 2018 while under twenty-four-hour armed guard protection. Clearly we have failed at saving them.

13th -"Frog Jumping Day": There was a time when there was a plethora of leaping going on, but no more, not since amphibian numbers drastically declined and in some instances were wiped out, as in the case of the golden toad, - last seen in 1989. So there's a pitiful amount of jumping or leaping to be jubilant about in this century. But it's because of their current situation we precisely need - a Leap Frog Day.

16th -"Love a Tree Day": Hear ye, hear ye...calling all tree-huggers. If people firmly grasped how trees absorb carbon dioxide and potentially harmful gasses, such as sulfur dioxide and carbon monoxide from the air and release oxygen back into it, which is our life buoy, everyone would stampede to the nearest tree and give it a squeeze instead of viewing tree-huggers as weirdos. Wildlife requires trees for protection, for building their homes, for nutrients, for scent-marking communication and enriching the soil for future vegetative growth. Trees provide life for all living organisms.

June

4th -"Hug Your Cat Day": This day will never get the number of followers a Hug Your Dog Day would, but I am a bona fide cat lover, and will eventually succumb to being a crazy cat lady, to which I'll be proud to be, therefore I will sing their praises. When I was a young child we lived in a city that had the Puss N' Boots canning factory just down the street. You could say it was in my blood, or at least in my nostrils, and perhaps I was predisposed to fall in love with the smell of cats and their food. Most people, when they think cats think of the small domestic types, but this day needs to celebrate the larger felids: lions, cheetahs, leopards, jaguars and cougars. Their numbers are diminishing - and recently the world wept when the beloved African lion named Cecil, was killed by a hunter. Trail cameras are a safe and effective piece of equipment to snap photos of these elusive, feline predators, and the books 'Ambushed' and 'Jaguar' - did just that.

14th -"Monkey Around Day": As someone who has worked with various species of primates, I can confirm they do like to play. Play is a major aspect of their social bonding, as are caressing, nudging, embracing, poking, kissing, grooming, and rough-housing. Their individual personalities are further broadened through inquisitiveness and self-amusement: - swinging, somersaulting, dangling, tumbling and tossing poop. Roll these all together and you have a highly intelligent, acrobatic simian. Be prepared for a taxing workout when you copycat their monkeying around.

29th -"Camera Day": Grab a camera, any camera, especially a trail camera, and let it shoot - stills or video of something moving through the bushes, or up-close, passing by. And try, for humble sake, to resist a selfie, because that practice is reaching narcissistic levels. You just might like the shot even more with something other than yourself in it.

July

10th -"Teddy Bear Picnic Day": It's a catchy children's song that my grandmother often sang to me, but it came to life for Dale and me when we checked our trail camera one summer's afternoon. Two bears sat snuggled next to each other, staring off as the sun sank. It was as though they were saying goodbye to a joyful day spent in the forest. With certainty, that photo would never have been possible if we had been present. The bears would have been scared off once they heard or smelled us. Those are the benefits and prizes we have gained by using trail cameras.

26th - All or Nothing Day": We've done plenty of NOTHING for our ecosystem's health - now it's time to go All-In to save this extraordinary planet we call home.

August

23rd -"Ride the Wind Day": Nothing knows the meaning of riding the wind like the kings of soaring: - the Andean and California condors and turkey vultures. They can ride the thermal currents up to heights of 20,000 feet and stay soaring without flapping their wings once, for hours. Seven hours without a single flap was once recorded for a turkey vulture. These buzzards of the sky created the term – riding the wind.

September

10th -"National Pet Memorial Day": Admittedly, it's a day you're not apt to feel festive, yet take solace knowing others share your grief. And though we all grieve differently, there's no question sadness is universal when an animal you have loved dies. For most, our pets die peacefully and humanely at the hands of a veterinarian, but for those who work in the field with wild species their pain is often linked to cruel acts brought about by humans. Dian Fossey and her beloved Digit, Gareth Patterson and his African lions, Mark and Delia Owen and their elephants, Dr. Lynn Rogers and his black bear Hope, - and Dale and me and the zoo's bachelor chimpanzee troop, which were riddled with bullets when they escaped their exhibit. Animals, domestic or wild, enrich our lives and touch our hearts in life and after death.

22nd -"Elephant Appreciation Day": Most people by now are aware of the plight of elephants being poached for their ivory. What makes their slaughter even more horrific is just how sensitive and bonded elephants are to one another. When a baby in the herd fusses, the entire family will rumble and rush to touch and caress the distressed infant. So, imagine when poachers approach a matriarch and her family, the emotional scars left on those that survive the butchering. For a simple piece of ivory jewelry or ornament, a family was split apart and suffering was all that remained. I must mention two books worth reading: - 'The Elephant Whisperer' and 'Modoc – The Greatest Elephant that Ever Lived.' Whether you are an elephant admirer or not, you will be one after reading those stories, after which you'll want to run out and get a T-shirt that says "certified elephant supporter."

23rd -"International Rabbit Day": It's a day to hail the essential prey animal. A rabbit's life is short and bound in stress. Even on this, their day, they can't be afforded the luxury of relaxing. Constant alertness and agility is what keeps them alive - for a while, at least. Safety is fleeting when you have predators in the skies and on the ground hunting you. These animals deserve high praise when they are able to awaken to another day. Most of our hare photos were blurred, confirming they are in perpetual motion.

November

16th -"Have a Party with Your Bear Day": As true bear lovers we say: Rejoice! But there probably aren't many that would, or could, claim to be personally involved with a bear - let alone prepared to celebrate a party together. But if you are one of those lucky individuals, say like; Doug and Lynne Seus, Casey Anderson, Charlie and Andy Russell, or are a caregiver to a bear in a captive environment, then bring out the party favours and whoop-it-up with these hulking mammals.

17th -"Take a Hike Day": Do they mean this figuratively in the annoyed, go-away-you're- irritating-me sense? Or literally: get off the couch and take a hike. We highly recommend an invigorating ramble on some nature trail, but make sure you have done your homework - mind and gear prepped for when you hit the trailhead.

All the former dates were simply a prelude to what I admittedly want to highlight.

March 3rd - I have placed this day out of sequence, because it rates a special earmark. Please circle it on your calendar. The state of our planet's wildlife has finally been paid tribute to with its very own day. In 2013, at the United Nations General Assembly, the Convention on International Trade in Endangered Species of Wild Fauna and Flora (CITES), proclaimed March 3 World Wildlife Day, to raise awareness and celebrate the world's wild animals and plants.

Since its conception, World Wildlife Day has gathered numerous delegates from around the globe to speak about Mother Nature. In March 2017, the theme was – "Listen to the Young Voices." If we are to halt the cascading die-off of our wildlife and wild places, we must include today's youth in the conversation, as they will inherit this mess. Their involvement is pivotal if we hope to turn things around so future generations have the beauty of biological diversity in their lives.

The following are excerpts from that World Wildlife Day.

Antonio Guterres, - UN Secretary-General: Poaching and illegal trafficking pose a significant threat to wildlife, especially some of the world's most iconic and endangered species. Strict enforcement of laws is important, but so too is awareness. As consumers, we have the power to demand that all wildlife products come from sustainable sources.

Amina J. Mohammed, - UN Deputy-Secretary-General: Over the past four decades, half of all wild animals and plants have been lost because of habitat loss, climate change, over-exploitation, poaching and illicit trafficking. Around the world, young people are playing an increasingly important role as responsible consumers and future conservation leaders to reverse this trend.

Irina Bokova, - UNESCO Director-General: The stakes are higher every day. Crimes against wildlife have been increasing over the past years, fuelled by conflicts and the trafficking of wildlife and wildlife products. The impact is devastating on the populations of both iconic and lesser-known species. Despite a range of decisions and actions, UNESCO Biosphere Reserves and Natural World Heritage sites have not been safe from these crimes.

John E. Scanlon, - CITES Secretary-General: World Wildlife Day is a very special day on the United Nations calendar. It raises awareness of wildlife conservation and it helps to galvanize national and international action. It is today the world's most important global annual event dedicated to wildlife. Our generation has not yet succeeded in securing the future of many wild animals and plants. To succeed we must fully harness the innovation and energy of youth, and combine it with the wisdom that comes with experience.

Bradnee Chambers, - UNEP/CMS Executive Secretary: At the United Nations, I work hard to protect migratory species. I want to ensure that future generations can still witness the world's great migrations, from those of animals that roam the plains of the African savannah and the swimways of marine turtles to the monarch butterfly and the characteristic v-shaped formation of birds in flight.

Dr. Jane Goodall, - Founder of the Jane Goodall Institute: All around the globe Mother Nature is under siege as human and livestock populations grow, encroaching into wilderness areas, destroying wildlife habitats, and illegal hunting and trafficking. With our burning of fossil fuels, over-use of chemicals in agriculture, industry and households, we are polluting air, land and water. We are suffering the effects of climate change.

Secretariat of the Convention on Biological Diversity: Wildlife is an important part of our lives. For many, it provides essential food and medicine. Ecosystem processes are driven by the combined activities of many species, and each organism has a role to play in providing us with economic, medicinal and scientific, recreational and ecological services, including cultural values. People are the architects of our current wildlife crisis, and people must be the solution.

"Listen to the Young Voices"- is about working across generations and connecting with young people on wildlife conservation and protection. It is about involving youth, as members of communities, in actions that will ensure a sustainable future for wildlife.

But urbanization and increased time spent in front of computers and on smartphones are separating young people from nature. There is a risk that these trends will undermine responsibility for wildlife conservation. At the same time, youth, with their enthusiasm and dedication to environmental issues, - can often provide leadership on these issues. The future of wildlife depends on proactively engaging, educating and connecting the next generation of conservation leaders.

A message from the founders of One More Generation, - Carter Ries and Olivia Ries (a young brother and sister team): We created this non-profit back in 2009 in an effort to help save endangered species and clean up our environment for at least One More Generation...and beyond. We believe that education is the key to solving all the problems of the world. If people were taught at an early age to care for all species on this planet and our environment, we would not have so many species on the brink of extinction.

Out of the mouths of babes! Their message was direct and succinct. Well done, and good luck with onemoregeneration.org.

CHAPTER 7

SHOULD BIODIVERSITY MATTER TO ME?

The Secretariat of Biological Diversity touched on this, but I feel it begs for more print space. We know we are not alone on this planet, yet we show a blatant disregard for how our decisions harm or impede the survival of all other species and the overall health of this planet. Although we are all individual entities, we are also interconnected, and how we treat this planet will affect us. That's the long and short of it. Our current and growing population numbers force us into a "use-up resources" mode to bolster our own species. We are stuck in the here-and-now mind set. These resources are not a bottomless pit - there is a finite amount to draw from, and we are nearing its end.

Giving less than ample forethought to the consequences or viable sustainability of our reckless actions toward other living organisms is what got us into this extinction pendulum that is swinging faster today than it was a decade ago. If we continue on this same beaten down path it will oscillate at breakneck speed into the next ten years. You could say we are imitating the ostrich by burying our heads in the sand (which they don't actually do, but that's another story).

We seem to go through our daily lives oblivious to how our world is dying around us, and the species that are dropping off like flies. Rich countries are the worst offenders - gluttonous consumers of our planet's resources. Multi-million-dollar electronics companies are masters at marketing their products, making us believe we need the latest version of phones. Take a moment to rethink that. Do you really need to replace your existing device? I hate to dampen your mood, but the moral is we need to stop living in la-la-land and wasting our precious resources on new and improved whatever's. Put down your phone, stop texting, and start doing.

I understand it can be overwhelming to hear of and see all the disasters, atrocities and brutality going on somewhere in the world every single day.

Maybe your way of coping is to not deal with it so you're not so depressed and can't function. You want to salvage some positivity and hope in your life. I get it. I do. But looking the other way, or turning the channel because you don't want to hear another awful story, is not the answer. Zero action will not return our planet and its biodiversity to its former glorious self. In all likeliness we will never reach that level again, but we must strive to come close.

Biodiversity is not unlike conservation. It's a word that's tossed around that you may or may not fully comprehend, and therefore you leave it to the academia's to decipher, hash over, forecast on and then simplify into terms the general populace can make sense of. Once given that data, we can apply it to a way of life that benefits or eradicates our world. That's what free choice has given us. Unfortunately what seems to be the trend is to disregard this bleak data and continue on our merry way, reluctant, and in some cases refusing to alter our life style even when it means wildlife and habitat destruction.

The "web of life" - is a well-known phrase that sums up precisely what biological diversity is. It's the resources upon which families, communities, nations and future generations depend - stock that can be drawn on. Every year, 100 million tonnes of aquatic life - fish, molluscs and crustaceans are taken from the wild. Wild game also contributes to food sources and livelihoods in many countries, especially in poverty-stricken regions. Additionally 50,000-70,000 species of plants are harvested for modern and traditional medicine worldwide. And you know what? Nature provides it to us all for free. In return, she asks only that we take care of her. Without question, we are not holding up our end of the bargain.

Plainly put, these resources are what apocalypse believers fill their underground bunkers with: - oxygen-rich air, a temperature-controlled environment, years' supply of food, drinking water, some heat source components, and garments. Now, imagine not having any of these reserves to fill the bunker. Essentially, the stockpile is void, as the world has been stripped of biodiversity - just a barren, dark land with no trees, no plants, no animals, stretching into the abyss. No doomsday conqueror will fix this mess, because it's not some movie or video game.

We've been hearing about the demise of the planet for decades. Back in the 1970s, alarms were raised about the rainforest. It's true much of it has vanished, taking with it countless species due in part to 'slash-and-burn' practices, whereby small farmers clear a few acres to plant crops or graze their cattle to provide for their families then move on. The coca, marijuana and opium trade has also decimated huge swaths of land by way of burning in order to plant. A staggering 5.9 million acres have been lost to drug production over the past twenty years in Colombia, Peru and Bolivia. Logging operations chop hillside after hillside to supply the world with wood and paper products every year. Every second, one and a half acres of forest is cut down, and every minute, the rate of deforestation equals the loss of twenty football fields full of trees. Topping the list as a timber giant supplier is our very own country, - Canada, at 31 billion kilograms. That's a lot of trees, and a lot of stark space left behind.

'So...to fell or not to fell: is that a straightforward question?' The answer is not a cinch. Or maybe it is, for without trees the land can regress into deserts as the domino theory plays out for all living things.

Dr. Edward O. Wilson, an award-winning scientist and biodiversity expert, estimates that 50,000 plant and animal species are being lost annually to deforestation. Peruvian forest engineer Marc J. Dourojeanni states that every year coca growers create a cesspool of contaminants by dumping 15 million gallons of kerosene, 8 million gallons of sulphuric acid, 1.6 million gallons of acetone, 1.6 million gallons of toluene, 16,000 tons of lime and 3,200 tons of carbide into the valley's watershed. What a sacrilege against Mother Earth.

If deforestation was to stop here and now, which it won't, whole groups of animals would still go extinct. Why? Once their habitat has been wiped-out, they die-off gradually in multigenerational extinction. It's not immediate or necessarily fast, but rather a fated death spiral.

Some question the dismal statistics and feel environmentalists too often cry wolf. This has created skepticism, for here we are 40-plus years later, and regions of rainforest are still intact. So did the environmentalists lie and get it wrong? It's hard to say, but what this news did do was lay the foundation for disbelief in the so-called 'habitat-analysis devastation' that is regularly quoted by the scientific world.

Let's put the naysaying aside for a moment and think about this. Asteroids and global warming are not the major potential causes of wildlife extinction that you may think. Habitat loss is the godfather of extinction. When animals find their homes destroyed, there is no point of return. They simply die. The International Animal Rescue Foundation summed it up in one sentence: - "Human growth + need for more natural resources + deforestation for grazing and food = land loss and animal extinction."

To feed our species requires a monstrosity called cattle. Livestock farming is responsible for many evils - greenhouse gas emissions being one. Its emissions today stand at an all-time high of 65 percent of human-related nitrous oxide. This represents 296 times the global warming potential of CO2, and it comes from good old-fashioned manure. Livestock also causes massive land assault, with approximately 20 percent of quality pastures gone as a result of overgrazing. Sediment becomes less porous and more compressed because of constantly being trampled, and erosion sets in.

Currently, livestock use 30 percent of the Earth's entire land surface, most notably pasture. Furthermore, 33 percent of the world's fertile land is exploited to produce the feed for the livestock. Forests are cleared to create new pastures, and in the Amazon alone 70 percent of rainforest has been turned over to grazing.

The livestock industry is the most injurious fraction of the Earth's escalating scarce water resources. It contributes to water pollution, eutrophication (an overabundance of nutrients - nitrogen and phosphorous) and the coral reef collapse. The major polluting agents are hormones and antibiotics, animal excrement, chemicals from tanneries, fertilizers, and the pesticides sprayed on feed crops. Pervasive overgrazing disturbs water cycles, which scales down restoring below-and-above-ground water sources. Also noteworthy are the levels of water extracted for the production of feed. Let's just say it's sizeable.

Meat and dairy animals now account for about 20 percent of all terrestrial animal biomass. Moreover, livestock's occupancy in far-reaching belts of land, along with its counterclaim for feed crops, chip-away-at biodiversity.

As resources are churned into waste quicker than waste can be churned back into resources, we've landed ourselves in a global ecological overdraft. We are depleting the very resources on which human life and biodiversity rely.

According to Mr. Steiner, executive director of the United Nations Environment Program in 2007, "The human population is now so large that the amount of resources needed to sustain it exceeds what is available at current consumption patterns."

The alarms are sounding once again, only it's not just about the rainforests. Each of us must vigorously seek out accurate information to ascertain what is happening locally and globally with wildlife numbers, habitat health and how we personally affect the web-of-life. We can't become defeatists. We can trounce this ruination of biodiversity and turn things around.

So, to answer the question: Should biodiversity matter to me? It shouldn't if you intend to take the next shuttle to Mars, but if that's not your plan, then it should matter a great deal if you wish to live a full life where food is plentiful, pests, disease and natural disasters are circumvented, and fresh water is not in short supply. Humans are currently using 25 percent more resources than the planet can sustain. We are losing species of plants and animals at a rate never before seen.

"It's time to Stand up for Wildlife. We can't just want it; we have to lay all our tomorrows on it." We borrowed these lines from the song 'Stand Up for Love', but substituted a few of the words to match our message. The lyrics are straightforward and say it best.

CHAPTER 8

CONSERVATION INITIATIVES

What is conservation, and what does it mean to you? Is it just a catch phrase, or do you embrace the notion? According to the Kids Encyclopedia, conservation is "the protection of things found in nature. It requires the sensible use of all Earth's natural resources: water, soil, minerals, wildlife and forests." How do you think we measure up to this statement? What I believe complicates conservation efforts and mires us in failure is the word sensible. Although we all know what the word means, employing it becomes problematic when met with self-interest, greed, ignorance and lack of moral conscience. Add to this already dismal situation the prevailing attitude that major charities often choose people issues over animal concerns. The level of caring simply isn't there for wildlife, no matter the impending catastrophe.

Life (all life) hinges on adequate habitat with life-support resources within that habitat. But that is vanishing, and it takes with it species after species. And as we know, the onus falls on us humans. Every 24 hours, 150-200 species of plant, mammal, bird and insect become extinct, according to scientists. Since science is still discovering new species, it's only an estimate as to what is out there. Nonetheless, a pretty good guess puts half of the Earth's wildlife species as having died off these past forty years.

The Wildlife Preservation Canada organization has a priority list to save less charismatic species, including snakes, lizards, toads, frogs, bumblebees, butterflies, turtles, rodents and birds that are at the brink of extinction. At present, what gets regular attention-time which shows just how extreme this species' numbers are becoming - bees. Without these pollinators, all of Earth's terrestrial ecosystems and the human race would not survive. Bees and less glamourous fauna are a part of our Canadian panorama. We grew up with them in our lakes and rivers, in our woods, on our hillsides, in our farm fields and in our skies. These species could disappear forever in as little time as a few years. Still, their plight often gets over-looked because the "wow" face of the polar bear is the one that takes centre stage in the media. It is the poster child for global warming, as it should be, but let's not ignore the others. Regardless of what animal is showcased, they all share the same threat of demise. So how do we stop the habitat massacre that's taking place at Mach speed, or at best find remedies?

I want to counterbalance doom and gloom with some hope. Currently there are strategies up and running. Y2Y, Freedom to Roam, Wildlands Network, Alliance for the Wild Rockies and Greater Yellowstone Coalition are some progressive projects that share the same mission: to connect and protect habitat. Certainly, it is easy to say, but their directives are not so simple to achieve.

Let's begin with Y2Y. It stretches from Yellowstone to the Yukon, so both people and nature can thrive. It has been hailed by the IUCN – World Conservation Union as one of the planet's leading mountain conservation initiatives. Canada and the U.S. have joined forces in this endeavour and formed a charitable organization. Multiple partners work collaboratively to foster conservation throughout the region and highlight and assist local initiatives that champion its large-scale objectives. These individuals essentially are conservation army ants. The list of involved partners is long, as it must be to paste together this vast landscape corridor - landowners, conservation groups, businesses, scientists, government agencies and Aboriginal communities.

Y2Y is not a new proposal. It has been around since 1993. Harvey Locke, a 35-year-old Calgary lawyer and environmentalist, had a radical idea to link protected wildlife areas to each other so species, particularly ones that traverse grand distances, like grizzly bears, could move safely between them. Four years later, Y2Y was officially established.

It stretches 3,200 kilometres (2,000 miles) along the Rocky Mountains through such national parks as - Waterton Lakes, Banff and Jasper, through Bowron Lakes, Yukon's Tombstone Mountains, Alberta's Willmore Wilderness Area, Montana's Yellowstone and various other reserves and national parks. The corridor weaves through inland rainforests, rolling hills, salmon rivers, mountain slopes, trout-filled lakes and alpine plateaus - a bonanza of rich diversity. Because of its massive, transnational vision, a variety of projects are necessary.

These projects deal with assorted matters: - private lands, policy, transportation, protected areas and public lands, co-existence, appropriate development, habitat restoration and promoting the vision.

One remarkable wildlife biologist went beyond just networking to promote the vision; he walked it. Karsten Heuer took on this unimaginable venture to learn firsthand what focal species like bears and wolves endure through the whole of the 3,200 kilometre trek. By doing so, he hoped to provide pertinent data to the organizations that were in the driver's seat of Y2Y. His gruelling journey armed Y2Y's top twenty-seven scientists with vital data that enabled them to map out how to protect core habitats, keep these habitats connected, and spur others to embark on similar work.

Unfortunately, it took years for the data, research, reports, traditional knowledge, existing land-use plans, and maps to be analyzed, and years beyond that to put things into play. By 2005 only the first cut of the Y2Y's Conservation Areas Design was finished. According to Heuer, "it lacks perfection, but is notable, for nothing else comes close." It coordinates the conservation efforts of many - land trusts, municipal governments, informed forestry companies, and others who work in remote areas.

Freedom to Roam is another heartening coalition created by the Patagonia clothing company. Their primary goal is to increase awareness of what wildlife corridors are and how they're a pivotal solution to wildlife's survival when faced with today's pressures from a disintegrating habitat, a direct result of human development and global warming.

Look around. What do you see - people and more people? As the alpha creature on this planet, we can wipe out most species by continuing on our current course of accelerating resource use and exploding population growth, or we can opt for life-style changes and action under the slogan, "Think globally, act locally." If wildlife species are to have a chance, they need our help - everyone's help. It can be in a very big or a very small way. Any way benefits - be it in your backyard, or a sprawling community green area. Wildlife is there; - we need only offer animals a degree of space to move through. When their life depends on it, do as the heroes in the following stories did. Get involved.

Two men slide their boat on top of the ice alongside a frantic deer that has fallen through. She thrashes and crashes into them, her eyes dilated with fear as her hoofs continue to break ice around her. She begins to slip below the surface of the icy water, but the men manage to keep her afloat by using their oars. As the jagged ice cuts into her body, the men know they must hurry. They position their boat in such a way that they are able to guide her toward the shoreline. She struggles to get her footing; - her exhausted, cold body shivers, but once on solid ground she stands fixed on the spot, not moving. Perhaps she is disoriented, or could it be she wants to share a moment with the men that saved her? The moment comes and goes, and she flees for the safety of the forest. The men could have easily allowed the deer to sink and drown and not thought twice about it, but instead they selflessly acted to help another in distress.

A brave individual approaches a snared wolf to set it free before it completely chews its own leg off. Whether in shock or understanding the person is there to help, the wolf remains motionless, looking up at its rescuer's face. Slowly and cautiously, the man opens the teeth of the steel trap. His strength is wavering, but the wolf does not move its leg. Does the man dare touch its foot? His arms start to shake as the steel trap fights against the man's strength to reclaim its victim. Finally, the wolf pulls his leg out and stands, as the trap slams down on nothing but air. The animal limps away, but takes one last glance back at the human who helped it before disappearing.

A great-horned owl is found hopelessly coiled in a barbed-wire fence, one wing badly broken and its body severely lacerated. The couple snip the raptor free and rush it to a nearby veterinarian. It takes months of rehabilitation but eventually the owl recovers and is released to fly the night skies once more.

In B.C., two bald eagles are entangled together at the top of a fifty-foot tree, hanging up-side-down, their talons jointly hooked. It is breeding season, and the males likely came at each other in a dominance display. The more they fight, the worse it gets - swinging violently, their massive wings flapping, doing nothing to relieve their critical situation. For three hours this goes on, and all the while the winter temperatures continue to drop, until the birds have reached maximum exhaustion and are hypothermic.

This was not going to be an easy rescue, but that didn't deter the onlookers. They notified a tree- cutting company, which immediately dispatched a truck to the scene. It raised the boom bucket up to the height of the distressed birds, unavoidably compounding the eagles' stress to get close enough to assist. Just when the worker was about to toss a tarp over the two to calm them, the birds, perhaps unnerved by the closeness of this person, stopped concentrating on each other and released their grip on their opponent. The crowd watching cheered as the majestic birds separated and flew off. In all likelihood, this scene would have ended with the death of both eagles had it not been for all those who cared enough to get involved.

An encounter with a glue trap placed outside a house left a long-eared bat covered in sticky goo. With its tiny wings helplessly stuck together, a group of volunteers lubricated the animal with mineral oil to break down the residue on its fur and wings. The bat recovered and was set free back into the area it was found. Many people are afraid to touch a bat for fear of contacting rabies, but fate put the right people in the right place at the right time for this small creature's survival.

A young female skunk was found severely emaciated and dehydrated and weighing no more than a kilogram. Death was about to claim her. She had gotten caught in a trap left unchecked for weeks. Her small feet and toes suffered fierce abrasions as she tried desperately to free herself, day after day. Luckily she was found and rushed to a wildlife rehabilitation centre, where she was compassionately cared for. Rehydrated and tube-fed hourly, her health turned around. Eventually she was released to live out her life, to spray her unique aroma onto others that might cross her path.

Something as innocent as chewing gum can be a death trap for an entity as tiny as a hummingbird. One day a family spots an object struggling in the tall grass. As they look closer, they find a bird stuck in a wad of gum. Its attempt to free itself is futile, and if help hadn't arrived, most certainly it would have been preyed upon by some stray cat. Its teeny heart pounds as they hold it in their hands and gently peel the gooey stuff off. They are mindful not to damage its delicate wings and tail feathers. Moments later, it sits perched on one family member's finger before buzzing off to a nearby tree branch. The children are thrilled to have been a part of such an honourable act.

One very dark and stormy night, two police officers were called out, not to attend a car accident, but to help a trapped deer. The more the animal flailed about, the more the soccer net entombed it. Its sharp hooves pawed at anything and everything to try to free itself. The rain pelted down on the deer and the officers as they cut away at the netting. As they cut, they kept a close eye on those deadly hooves, quite capable of disembowelling them. It took several tries to get the net clear of the animal, but the blowing wind finally helped fling it free of the deer. It bounded away, not looking back, but no doubt grateful to be freed.

None of these wildlife heroes got involved because they expected a glory parade, or some reward, or even a thank-you. They simply let their hearts lead them to help another that needed help.

For some, the term habitat loss means next to nothing. If there are fewer wildlife species, big deal, for it has nil impact on their daily life - they simply don't care. As long as they have their cellphone attached to their body 24/7, they are apathetic about global issues. If anything they believe whole-heartedly that any available land should be industrialized, grazed, mined, logged, drilled, pipelined and bulldozed. But to us and others, this would be a travesty to allow even one more species to vanish. Our planet is spectacular because of the diversity of the species that live within our ecosystems, not the commercialization of it. Sure, life will go on for us homo sapiens regardless, but might we not lose our quality of life if we lose what thrills us, urges us to seek answers, forces us to learn new adaptations, quenches our thirst for new discoveries, plunges us to the edge of our own fears and mortality, and moves us to action. That's what will happen if we destroy the very thing that makes us feel alive and enriched.

When you hear an autumn leaf free-fall from its host, and your nose picks up the pungent smell of decaying vegetation on the forest floor, and your eyes spot a faint movement on the tip of a branch, then and only then, will the well-hidden secrets of the trees reveal themselves? A walk in a city park holds no mysteries, but I suppose if you're staring down at your iPad or iPhone you're not looking for any rousing mysteries. What a shame!

Stories of cruel, depraved acts inflicted upon wildlife are also out there, but we chose to omit them. Those who embody the benevolent side of humanity deserve to be mentioned, for it is they who carry the torch for positive change and sustain hope for our planet's future, for all species. You restore our faith in the human race when we hear of your intervention to save an animal in distress.

Every day, new trails are sliced through the back-country as humans seek a break from our technologically-driven lives, and it is there that hikers, bikers, skiers and campers could confront something that propels them into survival mode. When that occurs, never forget you are in the home of wildlife. Be respectful and aware of your surroundings.

With seven billion of us on this planet, imagine what gains could be made if every one of us chose to do just one thing to protect wildlife every day. Even the smallest action can have a big impact. You ask, "But what can I do to help; I'm only one person?" Boyan Slat could answer you best. He is a 22-year-old Dutch entrepreneur, inventor and aerospace engineering student who endeavours to clean plastic waste from the world's oceans. He is an inspiration, proof that one person can work wonders.

If you take on just one of the following you'll make a difference, and when you do don't be afraid to let loose. Be silly and unencumbered and dance the Wildlife Warrior swagger. It will make you feel wonderful.

Ten Keystones To Save Wildlife

1. **Adopt**. Rally your classmates together to adopt an animal from a wildlife conservation organization such as the World Wildlife Fund - Canada, Jane Goodall Institute, Whale and Dolphin Conservation Society, Boreal Songbird Initiative or your local zoo.

2. **Join**. Whether you're into protecting natural habitats or preventing wildlife trafficking, find the organization that's at the heart of your passion and get involved. Become a member and stay informed. There are so many to choose from: - Great Bear Rainforest, Nature Conservancy, Roots & Shoots, Defenders of Wildlife, Wildlife Preservation Canada, Hope for Wildlife, and Canadian Wildlife Federation, to name but a few.

3. **Visit**. Provincial or national parks, wildlife refuges, zoos and aquariums are all home to wild fauna. Open your mind and learn about our planet's species from the professionals while experiencing Earth's most amazing animals up close.

4. **Chip In**. Pick a cause and support it. Twenty-square-feet of forest can be saved by making an online contribution. It will fend off deforestation. And if

you visit a zoo or sanctuary, don't begrudge paying the entrance fee. Your dollars help maintain these key conservation facilities.

5. **Volunteer**. If money is an issue, then give of your time. Most zoos, rehabilitation centres and organizations offer volunteer programs. In fact, they rely heavily on volunteers to meet their mission of caring and preserving our planet's flora and fauna. You could help rescue, heal and release an injured animal and even educate visitors. Whatever you choose, roll up your sleeves and get to work.

6. **Duty-bound shopper**. Refuse to buy products made from endangered animals or their parts and by doing so you shut down wildlife trafficking from being a profitable enterprise. Bear gallbladders are a prime example of the animal being killed for the sole purpose of harvesting its organs for fake medicinal properties. Stop this savagery. In addition and this is an easy one, endeavor to trim your grocery list and waistline by consuming less beef. It furthers the fight against deforestation - less clear-cutting for cattle grazing.

7. **Jump In**. Garbage isn't just unsightly, it risks the lives of birds and other animals that get their necks strangled in the plastic rings or eat the plastic bags. Fish, turtles, dolphins and whales get mercilessly entangled in nets. A recent news story showed a dead pilot whale whose necropsy recovered over eighty plastic bags from its stomach. That's an atrocity. Small fish ingest small particles of these plastics, in turn getting eaten by larger fish, which we humans then catch and eventually consume. Essentially, we are eating the very plastics we initially threw away. Its karma, wouldn't you say? Put garbage where it belongs, or better yet, reduce the garbage you create.

8. **Recycle**. Find innovative ways to use things you already own. Resist the new-and-improved impulse of today's culture. Those discarded, disposable items end up in our landfills, and they don't decompose. Pick products whose packaging is minimal. Even mail manufacturers urging them to use eco-friendly products. Consider recycling your mobile devices to reduce the demand for the mineral coltan, which is mined in lowland gorillas' habitats.

9. **Restore**. This one is vital, since 85 percent of all threatened and endangered species are in that situation because of habitat destruction. A counterblow to this situation is to plant native trees, or wild flowers for the bees, or restore wetlands, or clean up green spaces and beaches.

10. **Be heard**. Don't be afraid to call upon your family and friends to do their part in wildlife conservation. Spread the word and make it go viral.

"To survive today, other animals must endure global warming, pollution and fewer habitats. More tragically, they must endure the silence of human hearts." – Anthony Douglas Williams.

Don't let this quote be true of you. Once you've read this book, we hope you will join us and others who campaign for wildlife conservation and habitat preservation. Don't choose complacency and consent to the status quo by leaving it to someone else to save what's left of our wild creatures. If you don't do it for the animals, then do it for yourself, because we are all connected!

When enough species are sliced out of the ecosystem pie, it diminishes biodiversity and the complexity of life, which throws everything out of whack and puts our own lives at risk.

There is an excellent example of this described by Matt Long of Landlopers: - "Sea turtles are one of the few animals that feed on sea grass. This grass needs to be constantly cut short by the turtles, and other marine life, in order to remain healthy. Recently there has been a decline in naturally occurring sea grass beds, which can be causally linked to the decline of sea turtles over the same period. These sea grass beds provide breeding grounds for fish and other marine life, without which they wouldn't exist, and many foods we humans eat will cease to be or exist in such low numbers that we can't harvest them. It's a chain reaction: - the lower-level fish disappear, which means that the middle and higher-level fish don't have anything to eat. So if the turtles go extinct, the cascading effect will be tremendous and absolutely will affect mankind."

Protecting all flora and fauna is a good motivator, if for no other reason than to save our own butts. To those of us who live the wildlife conservation mantra, it takes on a deeper meaning. Their beating hearts join our beating hearts in a song of joy - the purest form of music.

So, the next time you chance upon, spot, hear, or come in close contact with any of nature's creatures, consider yourself blessed. And in that instant, place your own desires second and replace them with compassion. Leave them be! Don't spook them, certainly don't chase them, and absolutely avoid getting closer to photograph them, no matter how nonthreatening you feel you are being, since you are not in their head to know what their comfort-zone distance is. All of these actions will force the animal to deviate from its mission to find food, conserve energy and replenish energy lost. Put plainly, - to stay alive. Give them a wide berth, as they have a tough job to survive in their shrinking spaces. For them, every day is uncertain. Don't allow them to be silenced because of us.

REFERENCES

Alderton, David. *Foxes, Wolves and Wild Dogs of the World*. UK: Blandford, 1994

Alderton, David. *Wild Cats of the World*. UK: Blandford, 1993

Ballard, Jack. Moose. Guilford, Connecticut: Morris Book Publishing, 2014

Bauer, Erin A. *Wild Dogs The Wolves, Coyotes, and Foxes of North America*. San Francisco, California: Chronicle Books, 1994

Bull, John, Farrand, John, Jr. *The Audubon Society Field Guide to North American Birds*. New York, NY: Alfred A. Knopf, Inc., 1977

Busch, Robert H. *The Grizzly Almanac*. Markham, Ontario: Fitzhenry & Whiteside, 2000

Chadwick, Douglas H. *The Wolverine Way*. Ventura, California: Patagonia Books, 2010

Fenger, Mike., Manning, Todd., Cooper, John., Stewart, Guy., Bradford, Peter. *Wildlife & Trees in British Columbia*. Edmonton, Alberta: Lone Pine Publishing, 2006

Haigh, Jerry Dr., *Of Moose and Men*. Toronto, Ontario: ECW Press, 2012

Hatler, David F, Nagorsen, David W., Beal, Alison M. *Carnivores of British Columbia*. Victoria, British Columbia: The Royal British Columbia Museum, 2008

Herrero, Stephen. *Bear Attacks Their Causes and Avoidance*. New York, NY: Nick Lyons Books, 1985

Hummel, Monte, Pettigrew, Sherry. *Wild Hunters, Predators in Peril*. Toronto, Ontario: Key Porter Books Limited, 1991

Ozoga, John J. *Whitetail Autumn*. Minocqua, Wisconsin: Willow Creek Press, 1994

Shivik, John A. *The Predator Paradox*. Boston, Massachusetts: Beacon Press, 2014

Silliker, Bill Jr. *Moose, Giant of the Northern Forest*. Buffalo, New York: Firefly Books, 1998

Smith, Howard. *In the Company of Wild Bears*. Guilford, Connecticut: The Lyons Press, 2006

Urbigkit, Cat. *When Man Becomes Prey*. Guilford, Connecticut: The Lyons Press, 2014

Van Ballenberghe, Victor. *In the Company of Moose*. Mechanicsburg, PA: Stackpole Books, 2004

Van Tighem, Kevin. *Bears*. Canmore, Alberta: Altitude Publishing Canada Ltd., 1997, 1999

Whitaker, John O., Jr. *The Audubon Society Field Guide to North American Mammals*. New York, NY: Alfred A. Knopf, Inc. / Chanticleer Press, Inc., 1980

ARTICLES

Be Bear Aware – *BC Bear Facts*

Canadian Geographic Kids – *Porcupine Facts Sheet*

Center for Wildlife – *Be Bear Aware, Bear Spray*

Cornell Lab of Ornithology – *Life History Common Raven*

Defenders of Wildlife – *Canada Lynx*

Environment - *International Animal Rescue Foundation*

Field & Stream – *How to Pick the Best Spots for Your Trail Cams*

Fun Facts You Need to Know! – *11 Interesting Facts about Wolverines*

ISCBC Plants & Animals – *Invasive Species Council of British Columbia*

L-P Tardif & Associates Inc. – *Collisions involving motor vehicles and large animals in Canada*

National Observer February 1, 2017 – *B.C. government admit wolf cull is inhumane*

The Nature Conservancy – *Pine Marten*

Nature Mapping – *Facts for Kids*

Pacific Wild January 20, 2016 – *Courts Asked to Rule on Wolf Cull*

Thedodo.com – *2014's Top Animal Rescue Stories*

Wikipedia – *Snowshoe Hare, Lynx, Common Raven, Coywolf, Coyote, Mule Deer, American Black Bear*

Wikipedia – *Yellowstone to Yukon Conservation Initiative*

Wildlife Rescue Association of BC – *Success Stories*

World Atlas – *World Leaders in Wood Product Exports*

World Wildlife Federation - *How does Biodiversity affect me?*

other wildlife related titles from HANCOCK HOUSE PUBLISHERS

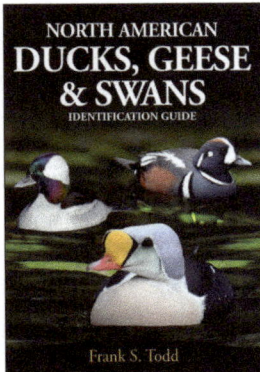

North American Ducks, Geese & Swans
Frank Todd
978-0-88839-093-6
6.5 x 9.5, 208pp
$29.95

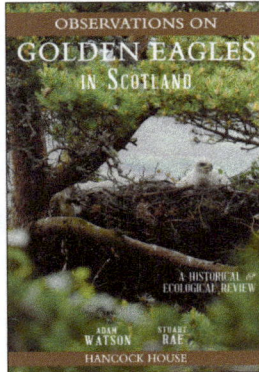

Observations of Golden Eagles in Scotland
A. Watson & S. Rae
978-0-88839-030-1
6 x 9, 146pp
$34.95

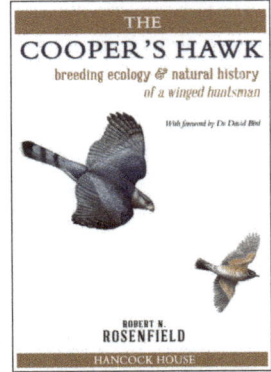

The Cooper's Hawk
Robert Rosenfield
978-0-88839-082-0
6 x 9, 164pp
$34.95

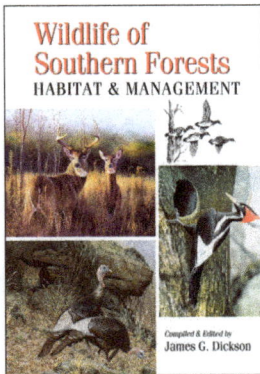

Wildlife of Southern Forests
James Dickson
978-0-88839-017-2
8.5 x 11, 480pp
$54.95

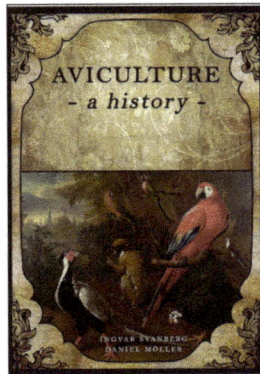

Aviculture: a history
I. Svanberg & D. Moller
978-0-88839-153-7
8.5 x 11, 268pp
$54.95

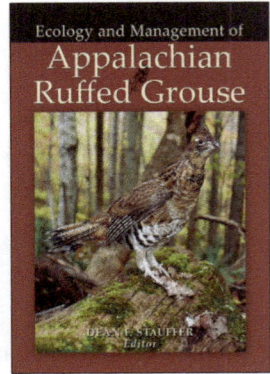

Appalachian Ruffed Grouse
Dean Stauffer
978-0-88839-667-9
8.5 x 11, 176pp
$49.95

HANCOCK HOUSE PUBLISHERS

19313 Zero Avenue, Surrey, B.C. Canada V3Z 9R9
#104-4550 Birch Bay-Lynden Rd, Blaine, WA, U.S.A. 98230-9436
(800) 938-1114   Fax (800) 983-2262
www.hancockhouse.com   sales@hancockhouse.com

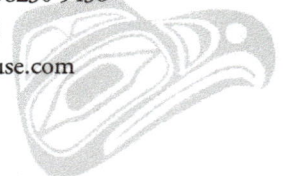

www.ingramcontent.com/pod-product-compliance
Lightning Source LLC
Chambersburg PA
CBHW040135270326
41927CB00019B/3396

* 9 780888 390585 *